AMELIA

EVERYTHING WILL BE ALL RIGHT

A WOMAN OF STEEL

A HEART OF GOLD

A SOUL MADE OF PLATINUM

A NOVEL BY Lyver MacRae

Library of Congress Catalog Card Number
98-91234

ISBN 1-57502-964-2

Lyver MacRae

AMELIA
EVERYTHING WILL BE ALL RIGHT

First Edition

Printed in the USA by

MORRIS PUBLISHING

3212 East Highway 30 • Kearney, NE 68847 • 1-800-650-7888

DEDICATED
TO
ALL THE LION HEARTED
WOMEN THAT EVER LIVED

Table Of Contents

Acknowledgements

The sources who contributed in the writing of this book have long been gone... My mama with her wit and love has been deceased since 1935. My siblings are gone too, I am the only one left, but...mama had left her influence that is deep-rooted in my soul.

The papers she had were lost in time – letters, copy of the manifest (a brief history of incoming aliens), birth, baptism – marriage certificates – gone.

Just the memories of telling me and confidences shared with me, all her heartaches and triumphs.

For years, too many to say, I was encouraged by my loving son, Jimmy, who cherished his grandmother and remembered her even though he was only eight when she died. "Tell the world about her wonderful life," he would say. So I set out to fulfill his desire to make her known.

Obviously, I haven't written all that was told to me, just fragments of an extraordinary life.

Her meeting and knowing Fiorello LaGuardia was a highlight she talked about often.

Unfortunately, I had forgotten much, but the love we shared, is as new, and alive, as the day I first laid my baby eyes on my mama.

I want to express my thanks and appreciation to my daughter Carolyn who co-authored this book.

The chore of getting the manuscript together – in spite of my illness, and mishaps, prevented us from publication sooner.

Thank you, my dear daughter, for all your determination and devotion you've shown me.

My sorrow is that my son Jimmy never lived to see this publication day. May he rest in peace and I know he is smiling down on me, saying, "Well done, ma."

My thanks and gratitude to you my dear grandson, Les, (Major, United States Air Force) for your advice, encouragement and your financial contribution toward the novel...

Without your helping hand it would have been impossible.

Your love is immeasurable – I love you.

My thanks also to my dear friends, Mary Quent Hayes and your daughter Joan Hayes Gane for all the time and love you gave in proofing the manuscript. Your help was invaluable. My love to you both.

And . . . I would be remiss in not mentioning the contribution Judy G. Smith of Tampa, Florida gave in getting the manuscript camera ready for publication. Her patience and diligence showed a professional touch. Thank you, Judy, you did an excellent job.

Lyver MacRae

Memoirs

A recollection of a journey Amelia took...as told to
Margaret...
Her lessons in love, compassion and forgiveness...
That led others to follow her little way...
It tells how she dealt with anger, hatred...
plus, the heartbreak of betrayal...
And...of the goodness that guided her to a reward...

PREFACE

To light a candle takes only one...
So...one does made a difference...
Because the light was lit, one could see...
And...the light they saw was love...

My name is Margaret Ann, the daughter of one such person...who's love was endless. She didn't light a candle so that you could see just her...rather, so one could see the Christ in her. This was my mother... Amelia. My beautiful mama... I shall never forget her...Her strength... Her heart, so full of warmth and tenderness... A soul the Lord had made for Himself.

I was told long ago that you have one shot of life in this world...so do it right. Period.

So...I ask you? Would you put this book down if I started out with... "Once upon a time?" If so...

I'll let Amelia tell you her story...straight from her own lips... Beginning with her parents – the beginning of it all.

Chapter 1

Beginning With My Parents

The Danube...the great river that flows through Hungary separating two cities, Buda and Pest.

My papa, Michael Andrews, was born on the Pest side, west of Buda. His family was religious, wealthy and aristocratic. Papa was the third child in a family of five, two of his siblings died at an early age.

They lived in the palatial row of villas at the upper end of Andrassy Avenue. Andrassy Avenue was the grandiose of modern Pest. The city ran the first electric underground subway line of Europe. Papa hoped to be at the grand opening when it was completed. He said it should be one of the "Great Wonders of the World."

God, art and history were his first love. That was until my mama came into his life. His love of her came second to the love of God.

My mama, Mariska Ann Nagy, was born in Miskolc, in the northern part of Hungary (pronounced Mish'Kolts, in Maygar language) in 1857 to an upper class family landholder.

Papa and mama met in the city of Pecs where papa was attending the University of Pecs. Mama was visiting her older cousin Anna and her husband Richard. Richard

1

was a graduate of that old university that started in 1367. And...the university was having a dance for newcomers.

Both Anna and Richard tried to entice Mariska to attend the dance. But...mama didn't want to go, she complained she hadn't anything to wear. Anna didn't want any excuses...

So...she gave Mariska her silk powder blue gown that matched her sky blue eyes – her black hair was shining. She looked gorgeous. Soon her eyes would glow when the night was through.

It was a difficult time, an almost impossible time for a young girl to meet a young man, outside of acceptable places. This to her cousins was an acceptable place.

There mama met her dream – my papa. It was love at first sight. He came over to mama and bowed, "May I dance with the most beautiful girl here?" Her face reddened when she curtsied, they said.

They danced every dance – not taking their eyes off one another. Soon they were dancing closer and closer. He put his lips to her ear and whispered, "Our encounter just had to be...we were meant to be together." He kissed her saying, "You will be my wife one day. I love you."

I was told that magic entwined their very soul, that the world existed just for them. And...with that feeling she answered, "Yes!"

This surely was a romance that would pale the love of Romeo and Juliet.

It was said that they had an affair of the heart that was so passionate that it seemed holy. Their devotion to one another was finalized by their commitment to each other.

This is the story told to us over and over again. My mama prayed that such a love would come to her children.

They saw each other daily. Their rendezvous included a chaperone – at the skating rink – at the outside garden restaurant – no matter where they went, there was the chaperone. But...that really didn't matter, for they only saw each other in their love world.

Being so much in love they wanted to be married and avoid a long engagement. So...Anna and Richard decided to help them.

Papa picked out a horse and cart to get their belongings to Miskolc to meet Mariska's family. And, of course, Anna chaperoned them.

Coming to the river, they took the barge, a flat-bottomed vessel that carried freight and passengers to Budapest.

Once in Budapest, they would board their cart and drive many miles to Miskolc.

Not too far off in the distance was the Czechoslovakian border. If one looked to the northwest of Miskolc, they would get a glimpse of the Carpathian Mountains. The mountain range was in Central Europe, extending from North Czechoslovakia to Central Rumania.

"The scenery has a grandeur all its own," he told mama, "it's breathtaking, just like you, Mariska."

Papa and mama were married in St. Theresa's Chapel, the same little chapel that mama was baptized in.

Within four years, they had three children, Jonas, Theresa and Mariska.

I was to come later...

Papa was a thoroughbred rancher. They came from all over to see the elegant Byerly Turk that was descended from one of the Eastern sires, a thoroughbred that was equal

3

to the Darby Arabian he had just purchased. These purebred animals were racehorses (Hungarian's love to gamble) and some were show breed stock. His stables soon became known throughout the region. Along with his wine products, I must add.

Mama became known for her interest in plants...not just any plants either...I guess you could classify her as an amateur botanist. She hybridized plants that were just exquisite. She must have had hundreds of those delicate Peonies that popped up in the spring. But she loved her Irises best of all; they were her pride and joy. She'd had to have that magic touch, because they showed more multicolors than they should have.

No wonder she became the official decorator for notable events and was asked to make floral tributes and bouquets for the statesmen's ceremonies.

We were fortunate to have such dignified parents that were cheerful and encouraging people. They prospered spiritually also and taught us how to be independent, above all...charitable in words and work. This kind of an up-bringing taught us also to be self-respecting, relying on everything and everyone that brought us closer to the Almighty.

Oh...yes, they were strict, but with their sunny dispositions, life seemed easier.

We made our Sunday Mass obligations (every Sunday) and had daily prayers at home in our chapel that papa built. Prayer will always keep us together, my parents would say.

My brother and sisters got along fairly well – you know how siblings are. Yet one thing was for sure, we all loved each other dearly. Mama and papa showed us how to love Jesus – and any time we felt angry or insecure or lonely we were to say a simple prayer. "Jesus, I love you." And...we were assured that everything would be better. This rule guided me throughout all of my life.

The Andrews family kept up with the news about the world; it influenced my parents' decisions on how to raise us.

It seemed every nation that touched our borders was at war, or wanted war. My parents diverted our attention by going about our daily work. We each were given tasks to do. We had laughter and love and music. Every night music...we all played an instrument. "Music," papa said, "makes the heart and soul happy."

But...I'm afraid our music didn't drown out the frequent news of war. Europe was in turmoil. Men knew they were soon to go to war. When my papa was called, he said he'd gladly lay down his plow to take up arms to protect his country and family.

In 1877 papa was inducted into the Austria-Hungarian Army and sent to Herzegovina. Leaving his beloved wife and two young children tore at his heart.

All through the Peninsula there were uprisings. It was because of the Anti-Ottoman movement. Russia declared war on the Ottoman Empire and counted on Austria-Hungary's neutrality.

That was a short war, thank God. It ended in 1878 with a treaty of San Stefano. That practically ended the Ottoman rule in the Balkans...it meant my papa could come home.

He came home in January 1878. And...Mariska was born November 1878.

Distraught at what he had seen, he vowed to work and pray for peace. Yet in the upper corner of his mind he vowed to fight to protect his family at all costs. If that meant he had to fight again, so be it.

Trying to put this out of his mind, he became a rancher again and tended to his large vineyard. Making time to be involved in civic matters was a must. He swore allegiance to his town, government, and, of course, his family.

Holding all these things in his heart, he would say, "Now back to the basics." So he gave his children a pony to care for. "How you care for your ponies should be how you care for every living thing, that's the basics of life."

Mama never seemed happier since his return. Life was good again. Papa was more tolerant and much more loving than before, if that could be possible.

Time had gone by and mama, loving my papa like she did, wanted another child. In spite of the doctor's warnings, she was expecting.

So...for nine months...mama took life easy. Everyone helped, even our neighbors. They all looked forward with love and anticipation to the new baby.

On a crisp sunny day...I was born...the last of four children in the Andrews family.

Born on February 23, 1880, I came a little sooner than expected. They told mama that I was too frail to live. But mama smiled and said, "This is God's Will, and His Gift to us that she should be born."

They named me Amelia Theresa, after my father's mother.

Soon after my first birthday, on March 13, 1881, the Czar Alexander II of Russia was assassinated by a revolutionary group called "The People's Will."

Papa was heard to say, "We will be at war soon, and if that happens, I will take my family to a safer country. Because this war will be worse than before...I will fight only when my family is safe and sound."

The whole family went to the chapel to pray for peace in our country.

Months later, it seemed as if our prayers were answered. For a while, anyway. On May 20, 1882, the Triple Alliance came about. Italy joined the Military Pact formed by Germany and Austria-Hungary. Now peace at last!

"Thank you, dear God," rang out in our land. Churches, synagogues and mosques were filled with grateful hearts, all thanking the Almighty for his intervention.

With the passage of time and the great expectations of war, we managed to spend precious moments with our family and making our vacations together memorable.

I remember going to Kekes, the Màtra Mountains, where we hiked the trails and fished...ate by the campfire, singing our well-rehearsed songs.

One time we sailed down the Danube River in our family yawl. It was a small two-masted sailing vessel. I remember papa turning to my mama and saying, "Mariska, do you recall the time we spent together on this river?" She looked up at him and had a big smile on her face, as if she held a key to their secrets. She winked at him saying, "Oh yes, Michael, I do remember."

When I saw her do that, I blushed. One never thinks of their parents as lovers. I remember thinking, "Will I ever find anyone like my papa?"

On our next vacation we were planning to go to Western Hungary, to Balaton Lake. That was a principal lake situated in Central Europe. We couldn't wait to go on this special trip. This lake was called the "Little Hungarian Sea," Europe's largest warm-water lake. My papa read to us that, because of Balaton's shallow bottom, bathers could wade out as far as 1,475 feet from the southern shore. He said that we would have to watch out for one another and "Promise me you will? Then we shall go." We crossed our fingers and promised...

We were all so excited about the things he was reading to us, we just couldn't wait. This will be the best time ever... We all will be together again, just like old times.

Janos was coming home from the university in Budapest. Theresa would be coming home from the convent school. Mariska and I waited patiently.

That night before our big vacation, we all gathered together at the supper table. Everyone was laughing and talking about the things we did together, and what we were going to do. All but me! Mama noticed I was picking at my food and I hardly ate. She scolded me for not eating saying, "There are people without food, so eat!"

"I can't, mama," I said almost crying, "I don't feel good."

Papa picked up on the conversation and said, "Amelia! Little one, go to your room and lie down. Perhaps you will feel better later." (He had a worried look on his face.)

8

I thanked my papa and after I had blessed myself, I was excused from the table. As I was leaving the room, I heard my mama say, "Amelia didn't look good today, Papa. I'm worried about her!"

When I reached the stairs to go up, it seemed that my foot did not hit the step. It was like I was flying. I must have taken four steps and found myself falling to the floor. I gave out a yell and everything went black. When I came to, I remember everyone standing over me. They all had a concerned look on their surprised faces.

Papa carried me up to my room and put me on my bed, kissed my check and said, "Amelia, everything will be all right." He stroked my forehead and I saw a tear in his eyes. "Little one, your brother has gone for a doctor."

When the doctor arrived, I felt much better. I wanted to jump up out of bed, then I heard the doctor tell my parents, "The excitement of leaving for your vacation could have caused a slight exhaustion, or she may be coming down with something. I'll give her some medicine to help her relax. However, I don't think she should go anywhere for awhile. What she needs now is sleep."

And...that I did.

Our rooster Henry woke me up (we had names for all our animals). Mama and Aunt Irene were in the corner of my room speaking real low. I heard mama say, "I cannot leave my little girl."

Auntie said, in a hushed tone, "I'll take real good care of her, don't disappoint the rest of your family, Mariska! Don't do that."

"Mama," I called out.

She came over quickly to my side. "What's wrong, my child," she said as she put her hand on my forehead.

"Mama, I don't think I should go...I don't feel that well. But I will feel worse if I make you all stay home with me. I'll be all right with Auntie. When you come back, you can tell me all about the lake. And...I'll go next time."

Mama turned to walk out of my room, saying, "I'll have to talk to your papa and see what he says." I sank into my pillow, hoping that she would've given me a little fight. Oh, well, we will see.

A little later my family came into my room. They all agreed I would be best off at home.

"Amelia, you will go next time," they said. My heart sank. I wished they had given me a little fight, and maybe stayed with me...

Papa decided since all the plans were made, they would go. My siblings were glad to hear that, but my mama was not. Papa insisted she go, so off they went.

Papa had lined up his finest carriage horses which he had trained and groomed for this trip in our elegant coach.

Why did I have to get sick? This would be the first time the family would use this coach for such a long trip...

"Dear God," I prayed, "help me not to be so envious, help them to miss me too much"...then I giggled. Silly me!

Not too many days went by when I started to feel much better. My cousin Ellen came up to my room every day to play games and beg me to go riding with her.

Then one day Ellen told me her father brought my horse, Lady, here (my papa named the horse for me). I loved Lady. "Come on, Amelia," Ellen said, "let's go for a ride." After that we went riding every day.

Ellen was an expert horseman; she mastered jumping over high fences and wanted me to do it too. "That's not for me, I'm too afraid," I said. Besides being an amateur, I didn't want to hurt Lady...

The day had arrived; my family will be home soon. I paced back and forth. I could hear them telling me all about that big lake and how much they all missed me. We'll hug and kiss, and kiss some more. Oh, I just wanted to see them.

Ellen was upstairs in her room...my auntie was preparing a meal for them. She was so happy cooking and singing. She was excited too. "They'll be so hungry when they arrive home," she said.

I was in and out of the house, anticipating their return. I had a million questions. This was the first time I ever spent away from my family. "I'll go next time," I vowed to myself, "even if I'm sick."

I heard the horse-drawn carriage. My heart raced and pounded so loud that I could hear it. "Here they come, here they come," I yelled out to everyone. I ran out to the path, only to see my Uncle Albert there. He looked awful, his face was twisted...he stretched out his hands and held me so tight. I became frightened...I never saw him like that. He was crying and shaking. We had our arms around each other. We stumbled to the villa. I was holding him so tight and crying, and...I didn't know why.

Aunt Irene came running down the steps in gaited leaps, almost falling. She screamed at him, "Are you injured?" She had a puzzled look on her face, as she looked him over from head to toe.

Then he blurted out, "They're all gone." Shaking his head he murmured about the carriage bolt. "It must have broken when they were rounding the bend." He then told us, he saw them fall to their death.

My uncle was pale and cold, yet the sweat was running off his face. Unbelievable tears poured out of his eyes. He kept repeating the same thing over and over again, as if he could not believe what he had seen. "Who? Who is gone?" My auntie kept saying. "Tell me?" By then she was shaking him. Afterward, some of the villagers came and told us that my family had an accident. They were all killed and their bodies were taken to the church hall.

There was so much commotion going on, I was so confused, and in a daze. The villagers were saying that the valley wind was too strong that day. Everyone knew that a wind ascends the mountain valley during the day. "Michael should have known that," someone said.

Auntie looked up to the heavens, saying, "He must have been too anxious to return home and didn't pay any heed."

A helper said my uncle was in the vineyard with him and yelled, "Look!" pointing to the valley path.

My uncle looked up and said, "It's Michael, oh, no!" He covered his eyes and fell to his knees, there was nothing he could do but cry.

That night my uncle withdrew to the stables, sickened by the tragedy. Aunt Irene, Ellen and I cried till early morning. Ellen fell asleep in the chair and I had fallen asleep in my auntie's arms. She let me sleep for a while, then it was time. When I awoke I thought it was all a dream.

My auntie kissed me and said, "Amelia, you must bathe and hurry to get dressed."

I asked, "Auntie, am I dreaming? Are all of my family dead?"

"Yes, my child, we must go to the church. You must be brave. Please, Amelia, be brave."

When I entered the church, I was still in a daze. It seemed like nothing was real. The candles were lit; it was so quiet...I saw many bereaved faces in tears.

Then I saw them...the five white coffins. I turned and ran out of the church. I didn't know where I was running to, but there I was, in front of a field of flowers my mama planted.

I stooped to pick the most beautiful ones, then ran back to the church; my face drenched in tears, salty on my tongue. Almost out of breath, I walked up to the altar just as they were going to close the coffins. I found myself looking at my family for the last time. I put one of my mama's prized Irises in each of their lovely hands, and then pressed it close to their rosary beads. With tears streaming down my face, I kissed each mouth for the last time...The impact of their deaths defied all reason.

Harsh reality grasped me for the first time. A pain stabbed my heart. When the priest was praying over the caskets, I realized I would never see them again! Never to hear their voices, their laughter, feel their touch, hold their hands.

The words of the priest echo in my ears even to this day:

"God, Our Father, we commend our dear ones to your loving mercy. We know that death is not the end but only a horizon that limits our sight, and that life with you is immortal and love eternal. Purify them in your love that they may see you face to face and come to the full enjoyment of your life and happiness forever. We ask this through your Son, Jesus Christ, Our Lord."

Then he blessed them with Holy water.

A very warm sensation came over me...my cold stone heart that was bitter over my loss began to feel life and love again. My beloved are immortal now and in the loving Arms of Our Savior.

I heard my papa's voice, "Amelia, just say, 'Jesus, I love you,' then everything will be all right. You'll see."

When they buried my family, part of me went with them. I stayed at the gravesite for such a long time, just staring into space and thinking of all the things we did together.

What fun we had...how I loved them! How they loved me! How I will miss them.

Then I felt my auntie's arm around me and she said, "Come, my little one...they are at rest now...and want you to go on."

CHAPTER 2

A New Way of Life

It seemed like ages gone by...the ache was still there, but I had come to accept my new way of life.

My aunt and uncle took on a new role of stepping in as my parents, and Ellen now became my sister.

Ellen was good to me...at first.

A number of times, she told me how bad she felt about the tragedy that took my family. She did everything to make me forget my pain. Almost everyday we rode our horses. She taught me new riding skills; I began to take more chances. I didn't seem to fear death or pain any more.

What a wonderful feeling it was to have the breeze brush by my face...my hair flopping in the wind. I actually laughed out loud.

It was hard to adapt to this new way of life without my loved ones, but I was trying, with God's help I'll succeed.

One day my uncle surprised me with a lovely piano. He said, "I remember how there was always music in your home. And...now this is your home, and there shall be music here too."

His words touched my heart, what a wonderful way to remember my family.

I tried to share my gift with my cousin Ellen, by teaching her how to play the piano.

Ellen said she wanted to learn, but soon boredom seized her, and she became weary of my lessons and annoyed with me! So I stopped tutoring her, and I played to please myself. While playing, the thoughts of my mama's voice came to me and it comforted me. She used to sing like an angel…and…now she is an angel.

I played for hours at a time, remembering my mentors.

One day, we were coming back from our usual walk in the meadows, when passing by a small lake we ran into mutual friends.

We were humorous and frolicking with each other when the antics almost turned tragic. They grabbed us and threw us into the lake with all our clothing on. Ellen, who was not a good swimmer, began to sink. She was spurting out water; it came out of her nose. Everyone was laughing at her, even me!

Then I realized she was drowning! I jumped back into the water and pulled her onto the riverbank…she was almost blue. I turned her over and began to pump on her back. She looked dead!

"Oh, Good Jesus, please help her," I cried out.

She immediately opened her eyes. Then she began to laugh so hysterically that she frightened me.

"I was dead! I saw myself going up to heaven," she said. "I saw your mama and papa. They were just standing there. They were with an angel.

"I looked down at my body…you were working so hard on me, to bring me back to life. Then I heard a voice saying, 'You must go back…It's not your time.'

"Amelia, you brought me back!" She began to kiss me and hug me so tight that she could have killed me.

My uncle came running down to the lake when he heard all the commotion. Going over to Ellen, he picked her up and pressed her to his face. He hurriedly walked toward the villa.

Once inside, my aunt was told what had happened. She took my hand and kissed it. She made such a big fuss over me...I saw out of the corner of my eye that Ellen was taking it all in and did not seem to like it...

After that incident I noticed that Ellen was gradually changing her feelings towards me. Was it because her parents gave me a great deal of attention? Does she resent that?

I didn't have to wonder any longer...because on one of our daily walks, she came right out and told me so.

My reply to her was, "They're my parents too!"

"No!" she screamed back at me. "You're not my sister! I wish you weren't here. My life has changed because of you...you've forgotten...they're my parents...not yours."

With that outburst, she ran back to the villa...

Stunned, I walked back alone and cried. It seemed I was always crying...

The following days Ellen avoided me without raising her parents' suspicions.

Then again one night at the dinner table, she was so sweet to me, treating me like I was her sister with her parents looking on in admiration. It made my stomach quiver.

I was so confused by her actions. I thought to myself, Ellen...can't you see how lonely I am? Why don't you love me anymore? But...I didn't say a word. I kept the hurt locked away in my heart. After dinner I went to bed and cried myself to sleep.

Ellen hadn't spoken to me in days. Then it happened again at the dinner table. Ellen smiled at me so lovely, saying, "Pass the bread, sister dear."

I had enough...I couldn't keep quiet any longer... "Stop it," I yelled. "Why do you hate me so much? Why are you pretending to like me in front of our parents?" I became very distraught and sobbed uncontrollably; my whole body was shaking.

Then my aunt came over to me and held me while I wept. She said, "We understand." But...before she could continue I pulled away from her and ran to my room.

I heard Ellen say, "She's a brat!"

With that I slammed the door and fell on my bed. I couldn't stop thinking of my sisters, and Ellen, and how we used to play together. We would sing our hearts out. We were inseparable...we did everything together!

Maybe that's it? She misses them too?

I found myself wondering why was I left behind? Did she also wonder? Crying again, I fell asleep.

In the morning I awoke with all my clothes on. I squinted at the sun shining so brightly in my room...I felt a new day, a new attitude...

I bathed and put on a real pretty dress. One I hadn't worn in a long time. I fixed my hair a different way. My thoughts of what had happened were pushed to the back of my mind, with the feeling that everything will be all right.

Perhaps they too had forgotten how terrible I behaved.

A gentle knock came on my door. Quickly saying to myself, I'll act as if nothing has happened. "Come in," I said in a sweet tone.

The door opened and my aunt bounced in with a spring to her step. She kissed me. "Good morning, Amelia, you look real pretty."

I looked into her happy face and saw her sad eyes. She took my hand in hers. "Sit here on the divan, I want to speak to you alone," she said.

"You know we all love you, you're family! Your uncle and I were talking about what we could do to make you happy. And we thought, soon it will be time for school. Just maybe, you would like to attend the same convent school your mama and I went to when we were your age."

"Oh yes!" I said in a pitched voice. "I'd rather not go back to the school my sisters went to."

I thanked her, kissing her so many times she started to blush. Then I told her my secret.

"I want to become a nun."

"What?" she said.

"Yes, I do," I replied quickly. I told her how I felt, how the feeling of security and peace comes to me when I am in church. "Don't you think that's why I was spared?"

"No! No, my child, I don't. It was not your time. Just like it was not Ellen's time. You have things to do. The Lord will take you when your task is finished.

"Now Amelia, let's go down to breakfast and we'll talk again later. I do love you child."

I didn't speak about being a nun again for fear auntie would try to change my mind.

That month I was enrolled in the convent. I was convinced that if any one could help me, they could.

The first day at school I made new friends, they came from all walks of life, different tongues and races.

My first few weeks were better than I imagined. Everyone participated in sharing work. We all seemed to stand shoulder to shoulder in all that we did. It reminded me of how my family collaborated in everything we did together.

What a joy to be here sang my heart.

The sisters were very optimistic in teaching us. And...soon I would tell them of my desire. They will help me...they will understand why I want to stay here and become a nun...

Most of the time my classmates looked happy. I did notice they wore fine dresses. I thought they came from the same family life I did. But they didn't. I was surprised to learn that some were poor and some orphans like me!

"Wait," I stopped myself. How can I say that? My aunt and uncle are my parents now! Shame on me. I'm not alone in the world like some of them are. I was never abandoned. I have a family!

Some of the girls told me that they even had a fugitive here at one time, who was wrongly accused of stealing. The nuns made restitution, even though the girl was innocent. She stayed until she graduated.

Another time a baby girl was left at the convent door. The good sisters found the child a loving home.

And . . .beggars that came to the door were always fed.

There were so many wonderful stories.

Like the time a runaway princess came seeking refuge. She claimed sanctuary because her stepfather wanted her to marry a much older man who had a very bad reputation. Besides being repulsive and disgusting, he was old enough to be her grandfather, for she was only twelve years old.

The good nuns hid the girl. And...after awhile the authorities stopped looking for her. The sisters found a haven for the young princess and her mother...and as the story goes, "They lived happily ever after." I loved the sisters and their fabulous stories.

There were girls here that were troubled; some felt deserted. I guess I was one of the lucky ones.

My aunt and uncle came every weekend and sometimes Ellen came with them.

This was my new beginning. I was full of hope and joy, learning that life was sweet.

I attached myself to an older teacher who's name was Sister Mary of Jesus (pronounced in the Hungarian way "Ma-rish-ka"). My mama's name. She was tall and thin, nothing like my mama. Just her sweet manners and lovely singing voice reminded me of mama.

We talked for long hours after school. She told me that she was a seamstress for Royalty before she became a nun. "When the Lord spoke to me, I said yes," the frail nun said... "And I gave my life to Him. And I have never been happier."

I remember thinking to myself, she gave her life up to teach us girls? I tried to understand.

Little did I know that she made clothes for anyone that needed them. Like the girls at the school, beggar's that came to the convent door, the poor who came every day for a hand out. How can she do so much? She sewed at night long after she taught us.

Sister Mary's old eyes were diminishing... but she kept on working.

I admired her and grew to love her a lot.

Sister Mary always said, "The poor will always be with us. We must help them whenever we can."

I thought to myself, "I'm too selfish to give my life up for others like this. How can I be a nun?" I went to the chapel to pray for guidance. I left the chapel without knowing.

The next time my aunt and uncle visited me, they insisted I come home for the weekend. When I saw the longing in their eyes, I said yes. It touched me so that I was compelled to oblige them.

After that I spent all my weekends at home and couldn't wait for my school vacations.

Being home was so wonderful. Ellen was sorry. She said she missed all the good times we had together.

Of course I forgave her...I loved her.

The years went by so fast and now...Graduation.

Sister Mary spent long hours teaching me how to sew and make beautiful dresses...time now to think about what I was to wear. I planned to make my graduation dress all by myself. Anyway...I had to.

Sister said, "No help from me, Amelia, you're on your own," then she chuckled and said, "Well, maybe I'll help just a little if you need it."

Then I was determined to do it all alone. It was a challenge. They had taught me many things, and that was one of them.

I excelled in my academic learning; I walked off with honors in the development of the Arts. I could spend hours in the museums, and I did.

But I wasn't ready for the real world. I wanted to stay here. Here with Sister Mary where I was safe. So I told Sister Mary that I wanted to be a novice (that's a probationary period for a nun).

Sister sat me down to talk (just like we did hundreds of times before).

"Your three years have gone by so fast," she said. "It's time for you to return to your family." Then she took my hand. She looked me straight in the eyes. "Everyone has a task to do." Smiling, she quoted the Bible, 'You are the light of the world, a city seated on a mountain cannot be hid. Neither do men light a candle and put it under a bushel, but upon a candlestick, that it may shine to all that are in the house.'

"Amelia, let your light shine before men, they will see your good works and glorify your Father who is in Heaven."

Pressing my hand, she said, "Amelia, feed the hungry, be meek and it will show your strength!

"When someone mourns, cry with them. When you see an injustice, feel their pain, speak out! Don't be afraid.

"Show mercy. Be a peacemaker. Have a clean heart.

"Help those that are persecuted unjustly, and when people persecute you, saying bad things about you, don't be angry! Remember what I'm telling you Amelia. Just live a good life, rejoice, then your reward will be great in heaven.

"Go out into the world, Amelia. Remember don't be afraid! You were taught what every young woman should know and what to expect from the world."

Sister Mary stood up straight, touched my cheek and poked my nose. And said, "You are a wonderful child, now it's time to be a woman."

She kissed my hand and my face, then in slow motion walked down the half-lit hallway.

Her frail body turned around, and with her hand came up in a blessing said, "See you tomorrow, little one, at graduation."

The strength she gave me was amazing. She taught me of what Jesus said...by living it.

That night I grew up!

This morning is my Graduation day.

Happy and excited faces filled the campus. Proud parents and relatives waited anxiously for the ceremony. Proper etiquette was the order of the day.

My aunt and uncle met me at the gate. With a hug, they said, "How proud we are of you."

Ellen, smiling, added, "You look so beautiful today, your dress is exquisite, so delicate…where did you get it?"

"I made it," I said modestly (it was a fine looking dress with lace and ribbons, not at all old fashioned).

"Amelia, are you serious? Is that the truth?"

She then told me briefly of her desire to be a dress designer in Paris, France. Then as if inspired, she said, "Maybe we can open up a shop together. Wouldn't that be nice, Amelia?"

"Nice?" It was nice to hear her speak about…us.

I managed to sneak away from them and the crowd. I had to just get away with my thoughts. I found myself in the garden, on an old familiar cement bench.

Alone…with memories of Sister Mary, and all of my friends, oh, how I will miss them. I was taken back in time to a birthday party the villagers gave the convent nuns. It was the celebration of the 100th year old convent.

There was a crowd, just like today. I could see it so clearly in my mind and hear the clamor ringing in my ears.

And the man that came running out of the crowd, screaming and cursing, rushing towards the chapel.

Sister Mary stood in his way to stop him; his eyes were on fire. His mouth was foaming; he looked as if he was a mad man. He cursed at her to let him pass. She extended her hand and said in a loud voice… "Stop! Begone Satan, leave this poor soul." Not a sound could be heard… the crowd waited… Horrified they stepped back…one could feel the hairs stand on end. The man fell to his knees

24

kissing her feet. He stood up straight...his eyes were shining brightly...he looked calm and serene. Peacefulness donned his face. I'd never seen anything like that in my life. I was visibly shaken, as was the crowd.

The people parted to let him go by...just like the Red Sea was parted. Sister uttered not a word, but walked over to the chapel and went inside. I immediately followed her.

Inside I found her prostrated in front of the altar. A ray of light emanated through the glass stained windows, directly onto the good sister.

I tiptoed out of the chapel, mind boggled at what I had seen. Could it be that Sister Mary was a Saint? I kept repeating over and over, I know a real live Saint!

Then I heard my name being called...Amelia Theresa Andrews...I quickly came back from my sentimental reminiscence of a past I will never forget.

I rushed over to auntie and sat down beside her. I grabbed her hand, pressing it tightly. She winked at me and smiled the biggest smile ever.

It was time to receive my diploma...I proudly walked up to the podium to accept my new beginning. I looked over at Sister Mary's face. It was beaming with joy. (Oh, Sister, you are proud of me. Thank you, Jesus.)

When all the diplomas were given out, a small reception was donated by the families. We had tea, biscuits and fruit. We laughed and told stories about each other. I was voted the teenage girl that giggled the most.

Then it was time to say goodbye to all our friends. I told the sisters that I would miss them. They hugged me and revealed that I would be missed too and assured me that I would always be in their prayers and locked in their hearts.

Sister Mary kept nodding yes, tears streamed down her face. We all cried and hugged each other and we vowed to keep in touch.

Now, yes now. I'll start my new life. I will no longer be afraid to meet the old world out there. They gave me the reassurance I needed...

Then walking away from them, the words of my dear papa rang in my ears.

"Trust...honor...and love, then everything will be all right...you'll see."

Chapter 3

Amelia Meets Joseph

Riding home we poked fun and talked about our new adventure together. Ellen designing the clothing for the wealthy, and...me sewing them up.

Just think we'll live in Paris, France. My head was swimming with grandiose plans for our future. (It was for that moment...I had forgotten what I have learned about caring for the poor.)

As we neared the elegant villa, I heard music and laugher. "What is that?" I questioned. "It sounds like someone is having a party." (Never thinking it was a surprise party for me.) No one spoke, but smiles crossed their faces. When we entered the house, there were throngs of people everywhere. It seemed like people were jammed in all the corners of the room.

The crystal chandelier illuminated a long table with all kinds of food on it. And...the most beautiful decorated cake I ever saw, with blazing candles covering it.

A shout of, "SURPRISE AMELIA," rang out. I was in shock. Wide eyed I exclaimed, "All this for me?"

Everyone from the village was there. People I hadn't seen since the funeral. It was so good to see all those faces again.

Ellen came over and hugged and kissed me... Introduced me to her new beau, Paul...then whisked him off to dance. Not knowing what to do next, I retreated to the kitchen. There I was comfortable.

My hands were busy helping the maids and the chef. I peeked out again, out of curiosity. My eyes searched for my aunt. All these people...

Oh, dear aunt, where are you? I felt frightened. As I was turning to go back into the kitchen, someone touched my arm. It startled me...

I looked up into a young man's smiling face. He was so tall and handsome, eyes blue as the sky, hair as black as coal.

"I was looking for you!" he said in a deep voice. "I saw you in the crowd, do you work here? What is your name?"

I didn't answer him; instead I ran into the kitchen and started to fill the platters to bring out to the tables...

I felt so foolish. Here I was working in the kitchen and the party was in my honor.

He stood near the door and would not let me pass.

"You didn't tell me your name," he said with a grin. He told me he was new in town and a friend of the family had brought him here.

"I'm glad I came...I found my princess!"

Smiling down at me again, he took my hand (I almost dropped the tray) and gently kissed it (I shall never wash my hand again).

I felt a warm glow all over my body and shivers up and down my spine. I thought to myself, is that what love is? Is this my Romeo? And cast my eyes to the floor.

Just then my aunt came in, "Where have you been?" she said in a troubled voice. "I was looking to introduce you to your guests."

The stranger excused himself and vanished into the crowd of well wishers.

Later I told Ellen all about my encounter with a stranger I described to her. Then asked, "Ellen, did you see him? Who brought him to my party?"

"He came with Paul," she said. "They're classmates, I think his name is Joseph. He'll graduate in a couple of months with him."

She didn't know anything else about him.

When the party was over, I thanked my family for bringing me so much happiness today. I went to my room with stars in my eyes and thoughts of Joseph on my mind (Joseph? Oh, I love that name).

Did he think I was a silly child? Will I see him again? Oh, God, I hope so...

This was quite a day!

Early next morning, a loud knocking at the front door abruptly awakened me. Looking out of my bedroom window I saw Joseph standing there. My heart beat with joy.

As I rushed to the head of the stairway, I heard Joseph asking my aunt for permission to take me out.

Oh, my God... My ears couldn't believe what they heard. My aunt questioned his intentions. She asked him about his family and what he wanted to do with his life. She asked him everything under the sun.

How can I face him now?

I heard my aunt take leave with him and coming up the stairs to my room. Hurrying into my room, I jumped into bed!

Rapping at the door, she opened it and called out, "Amelia, are you up?"

"Yes, auntie," I said rubbing my eyes.

"You best get dressed, you have a caller," she said. "And wear your pretty green dress! It's Joseph, so don't keep him waiting! He seems anxious to see you."

Coming into the room where he was, I acted surprised! There he was...with that adorable grin on his face.

He came toward me. He bowed, picked up my hand and gently kissed it. "I thought about you all night," he said.

I looked over at my aunt and she smiled, saying, "I'll leave you alone now, but remember, Joseph, what I told you!"

"What does she mean?" I said to him. He didn't answer me. He just smiled.

He leaned down and whispered, "So...your name is Amelia? What a sensuous name you have."

The sound of his voice gave me chills.

"Come with me," he said, and he showed me a luncheon basket. "I hope you have a big appetite, I have plenty of food to eat." (His grin almost devoured me.)

"My buggy is awaiting you, princess."

We went down to the lake and he stopped near one of my favorite trees. He set a blanket down and beckoned for me to sit down (I was so nervous that I was trembling at the thought of being close to him). I tried to hide my excitement like a schoolgirl, but silly giggles every now and then gave me away. He must have realized that I was very shy and inexperienced at this sort of courting...any courting for that matter.

So he took the basket and started to take the food out, saying as he did, "You're the princess and I am your servant."

After we ate everything in sight, he stretched out on the blanket and stared up into the blue sky. A very sad distant look came over his face, as if he were in a trance. He began to tell me all about his life.

"We had a beautiful family, and then it all came to an end." He choked up, blinked his eyes, and continued to tell me of how he lost part of his family to an epidemic that swept Europe years ago.

"It was hard trying to keep the rest of the family together. We made a pact...that my sister and brothers would always stand by each other forever, no matter what.

"I held two jobs, one at the university helping the professor grade papers and the other on a railroad network. The railroad work was backbreaking but worth it. With that money I managed to save enough to go to night school at the University of Budapest.

"They had a class in Foreign Policy and I wanted to become a foreign diplomat. But I changed my mind later. Budapest is the center of learning," he said with enormous pride. I could not help but see the boy in him as he spoke. His cheery optimism for the future made me smile. He saw a funny grin on my face and it made him feel self-conscious, so he changed the conversation.

"I have brothers, you know. They're saving for a piece of land, they want to grow grapes and have a large orchard. I guess we all had a lot of dreams. I wanted to be a soldier and join the war, but – it soon ended." He couldn't stop talking; he went on...

Then he gave me another history lesson about the war.

31

He looked at my smiling face. His face reddened, then he broke his story telling and said, "Enough about me. What about you?"

So, it was my turn…

After I told him how I came to live at my aunt's home, he put his arms around me and said, "We sure do have something in common. We have a bond, Amelia! Our families broke up because of tragedy."

We held each other for such a long time, listening to our hearts beat.

We knew what heartbreak felt like…the sword had pierced our spirits and we were wounded. Words didn't matter.

Joseph looked up at the sky. The clouds were starting to cover the sun. "Time to go," he said, but then added, "I must see you again! Tomorrow?"

I nodded yes!

Is he going to kiss me now? My lips quivered. Instead he hurried me to the buggy.

"Can't get your aunt mad at me for keeping you out so long." As he said that, he had a twinkle in his eyes.

The ride home was quiet except for the sounds of the huffs and crackling of the buggy wheels, and…the beating of my heart.

When Joseph brought me to my door, he kissed my hand. Gently brushing back my hair, he said, "Goodbye, my love…"

"See you tomorrow?"

I shut the door in a dream…could this be happening to me?

Just as I was mounting the stairs to my room to finish my dream, my aunt showed up with a big smile on her face.

"How was your picnic, sweetheart?" she said.

I must have been beaming when I said, "Just heavenly, my love," as I floated up the stairs.

Tossing and turning half the night, I couldn't wait for morning to arrive. Over and over in my mind I kept reliving the picnic and all we had said to each other. Dare I dream that this time he would kiss my lips? How bold I am, I thought, then fell asleep.

In the morning I scrambled to get dressed quickly, hoping he would come early. I peeked out the window a hundred times. When will he come? Will he come? So many questions.

Then he appeared...My heart pounded so loud I could hear it. Could anyone else hear it? I almost felt ashamed.

I didn't wait for the houseman to open the door. I ran down the stairs, two steps at a time. Just before he knocked, I opened the door and said in a surprised voice, "Oh, Joseph?"

"Amelia, you look so beautiful." He put his hands on my shoulders and pulled me close to him. He tenderly kissed my cheek. I felt the heat come to my face.

Ellen came to the door and said, "Why don't you ask Joseph in?"

She said she was waiting for Paul to arrive, they were going horseback riding. Then added, "Come along with us, we'll have fun."

Joseph looked at me with a yes in his eyes, so I said, "Yes, that sounds like fun. All right, Joseph?"

When Paul arrived, he came into the sitting room and with a loud voice said, "Let's go, Ellen."

"Wait, Paul," Ellen said sweetly, "the houseman is bringing us something cool to drink. And then we'll all go...Amelia and Joseph are joining us."

When the beverage arrived, Ellen took the tray and served us. Laying the tray down, she hastened to bring Joseph's drink to him. You could hear the rustle of her riding skirt as she scurried to his side.

She looked up at him and said, "My, you are tall!" bringing her body close to his, she giggled. He leaned down to her, as if he was going to kiss her. Instead he whispered something to her.

It was plain to see he was enjoying her wit. I had to do something real fast to break her spell. "Well, let's go," I said, as if working against time and feelings.

We walked to the stables. Joseph held my hand; he didn't speak, he just had a smile on his face, one I didn't recognize. It was as if he was thinking of what just happened, and was basking in her dazzling and alluring charms.

To me... my cousin acted like a real hussy, and Joseph...liked it! I felt so jealous of her...and was envious of how brazen she was.

Did I show my feelings too much? Did Joseph notice my uneasiness? I must try to hide these awful emotions. This trait is not flattering to my person. Joseph will see it. He may think of me as a very small person. Dear Jesus, please help me. Jesus, I love you...

On the path, Joseph and I started to have real fun; we laughed and rode side by side, taking in our surroundings. Ellen and Paul were in front of us. When all of a sudden I saw Ellen kick the ribs of her horse with her spur. It was so hard that her horse flew speedily away.

Ellen screamed, she was pretending she could not control her horse...

Little did Joseph know Ellen was an expert equestrian.

Now…I knew she was shamelessly flirting with him.

Joseph zipped past Paul to catch up with the (supposedly) run-away horse. When he caught up with her, he snatched Ellen up off the horse. And the horse rode off…

Ellen grabbed Joseph and told him he saved her life. She put her arms around him and kissed him for such a long time (I noticed he didn't push her away).

When we rode up to both of them, Paul was angry and he showed it…he actually yelled at Ellen and told her to ride on the back of his horse to the stables.

Ellen looked back at Joseph, smiled, and climbed onto Paul's horse. They rode off in full gallop.

Paul was infuriated. It frightened me…

"That was a brave thing you just did, Joseph," I said.

He just shrugged his shoulders in a gentlemanly manner.

On our way back to the stables, I asked him…with hesitation, "Would you like me to act like my cousin Ellen? You seem delighted with her."

He said with annoyance, "No, Amelia, I love you just the way you are…"

"Tomorrow? May I see you tomorrow, Amelia?"

He unsaddled the horses, never saying a word and left without kissing me goodbye.

My heart sank. What is he thinking about? Does he really like Ellen better than me? What will he say tomorrow?

I didn't see Ellen that night. Auntie said that she went to dine over at Paul's house. And in the same breath, said, "Where's Joseph? I have a lovely dinner here for the two of you."

"He had to leave," I said, as I sat down to the dinner table with my aunt and uncle.

They both looked at each other then said grace.

My uncle started a small conversation with me, but I didn't answer him. Instead, I just picked at my food and said I wasn't hungry. So I excused myself and went down the long hall to the chapel.

I always went there when my heart was full. I needed a compassionate ear and a solution to my woes. I knelt before Our Lady's statue and lit a candle...I prayed for her to ask her Divine Son, Jesus, The Light of the World, to guide my steps and help me to make the right decisions about my life.

Sister Mary used to say, "Trust your judgments, then do it, but...do it right!"

As I looked up into Mary's face, the flicker of the candlelight made Mary seem as if she was smiling at me...

It was as if she was saying what papa used to say. "Don't worry, Amelia, everything will turn out all right..." I blessed myself and went upstairs to bed.

In the morning I heard the birds singing. Then my heart started to sing...then I started to sing too...out loud.

The sun was just coming up. My first thoughts were of Mary, the Mother of God...I saw her smile again in my mind. Saying, yes, everything will be fine...trust...and love...

Then I heard a light tap on my door. It was my aunt. "Sleepy head, get up," she said. "Joseph is downstairs waiting for you. Don't forget to dress pretty."

As I hurried to dress, I stole a look in the mirror a thousand times...each time I saw my flaws.

Too late to change my looks, dear Lord, I thought. With that in mind, I hurried.

Reaching the landing step, I heard my aunt say, "Do come back real soon, and God speed."

She left the room as I entered. Her face showed strain.

Joseph had his back to me; he was looking at my picture on the mantle. He didn't hear me come into the room...his mind was in a distant place...I touched his arm, and he swerved around and grabbed me...kissing me so passionately that it took my breath away. The emotional response I felt was overwhelming. I held him so tight. We held each other and kissed and kissed.

Then he looked into my eyes. "Amelia, I love you, will you wait for me?"

"Joseph, where are you going?" I asked.

"My love," he said, "I had signed up to fight in the Turkish Army. It was long before I met you. I must keep my commitment. Amelia! I signed papers...do you understand? This is tearing me apart." Tears streamed down his face.

"Oh, no! No! Joseph?" I said. I pushed away, and he drew me close to him, saying, "I love you, love you!"

"You didn't answer me, Amelia, will you wait for me?"

I said in an angry voice. "What if you get killed?"

He kissed my lips, saying, "I'll be careful, I'll come back to you, I promise, Amelia, I promise." He then took me into his arms again.

Lost in his embrace, I whispered in his ear, "Yes, Joseph, I will wait for you, my love."

"You won't be sorry, Amelia, I'll make you happy. I want to marry you, I truly love you."

We spent the good part of the day planning his return...he had so many dreams, dreams that included me.

"Amelia? I'll be back before the planting starts next year. Amelia, please keep that in your heart. And pray for me...I promise you I will return soon..." His breath quickened, "I love you...I love you."

From the look on his face and the touch of his hand against mine, I knew it was true.

He then left me with my heart palpitating so that my breast vibrated. I watched him, as he became a speck riding down the path.

Frozen in my shoes, I managed to shut the door behind me. Leaning against the door I wondered...what would I do without him? Will I lose him like I lost the rest of my family?

Again I found myself in the chapel on my knees. There I asked the Virgin to pray for us and keep Joseph safe. "Please have him come back to me. Please ask Jesus to alleviate me from all this pain. Jesus, I love you, Jesus, Mary and Joseph, I love you."

No sooner had I said that prayer a certain calmness came over me. My inner voice told me it would be all right.

I knew it must be my papa. The Virgin always lets me hear his wonderful voice.

Chapter 4

Getting Away

Days later Ellen came to me, saying she was sorry for her behavior. "I'm ashamed and regret what I've done to you, Amelia." Her eyes glued to the floor, she continued, "I knew how much I was hurting you. I don't know what came over me. I knew you loved Joseph, still I wanted to take him from you...Please forgive me. You know I love you, I always have!" She leaned over me caressing my face.

"You're a good god-like person, Amelia, I know there's no revenge in you and you'll forgive me. I'm counting on it!"

She kept shaking her head, saying, "I feel that I should be punished."

I answered her with my arms around her. "I did resent you and almost hated you, Ellen. But...no I couldn't do that...because love got in the way...You're my sister. Besides, Ellen, I'm really too worried about my Joseph to think of anything else."

"What's wrong with Joseph?" Ellen asked.

"He's going off to war. I may never see him again." I could not hold back the tears. "There's no bitterness in my heart for you, Ellen, only love."

We said we would never hurt each other again, and to be there for each other in time of need.

We were closer than ever before.

The following week Ellen came to me, she was extremely nervous. "Paul and I have broken up. I don't ever want to see him again, he's cruel and evil," she said.

I shrugged it off as lovers' quarrel and told her so. "Ellen, don't worry you'll get back together again."

"No!" she shrieked, "he attacked me! But...I managed to run away from him."

I took her arm, "Ellen! Did he?"

She turned away from me as if ashamed. She broke into tears, "He said he always gets what he wants."

She put her hands into her face...her words and actions seemed to validate what I was thinking...

"Oh, my poor Ellen," I said.

She looked at me, "Amelia, he's bad, he says he wants you next. He's despicable, stay away from him!"

Ellen was shaking. "I'm afraid to tell our father, if he knew he would kill him."

I held her hand. "Come on down to the stables and we'll go for a ride to ease your tension. We'll decide what we will do later."

After our ride back to the stables, we still didn't figure out what we should do. We decided we'd leave it for another day.

After we anguished over what we would do...and how to do it. Ellen said she had to lie down and left me to unsaddle the horses.

As I was pulling the bridle over the horse's head, I heard a noise. I turned around to see Paul standing there.

He had a friendly smile on his face. He politely asked if he could help me.

I stammered back in a low voice, "No thanks!" I knew he sensed that I was uneasy, so he backed away and walked to the door as if to leave.

But instead he shut the stable door.

He walked over to me and put his arms around me and started to kiss me. I pushed him away and he slapped me so hard that I was knocked to the floor.

"Now... I got you where I want you!" he said. "You'll love it," he panted, as he frantically pulled on my blouse and tore my clothes half off.

I screamed and he hit me again. "Keep quiet!" he said. I started to scratch his face and I bit his lip. I could taste his blood. I managed to get up... He punched me again... I went down, and then he jumped on me...I was so weak with fear and so helpless that I stopped fighting him.

He said in a raspy voice, "You're going to be mine!"

I shut my eyes and whispered loudly, "Jesus, Jesus, I love you, help me."

All of a sudden he stopped tearing at me. He looked at me, and an astonished look came on his face...he became pale, as if he had seen a ghost.

"You?...You're an angel?"

Mysteriously, he sprang off of me! His eyes were almost popping out of his head.

I lay frigidly on the hay and dare not move for fear of him.

Half dressed, he struggled to his feet. "I'm sorry, sorry, dear God, forgive me!" he wailed. He ran out the stable door, right into my uncle, almost knocking him over.

"What's wrong, Paul?" my uncle yelled at him as he scurried away. Then my uncle looked into the stable and saw me lying there. I was half clothed, my mouth and nose bleeding.

He ran over and helped me to cover up. "What did he do to you?...Oh, my God, I'll kill him!"

He started to go after him...I held his arm, saying, "I'm all right, he didn't touch me that way."

With a sudden gust of breath, my uncle stood up. "I'll get help...you'll be taken care of."

As I was lying there, I saw the vein in his neck pulsate as he said, "Stay here, my child, wait for auntie."

When he reached the villa, he yelled, "Irene, go to Amelia quickly, she's in the stable...she's hurt."

Then he went over and unlocked the gun case and took out a pistol.

Overwrought with anger, he rode like a madman to Paul's house. Paul's father was out in front with two hired hands. He tried to stop my Uncle Albert.

But my uncle jumped from his horse without having the horse come to a full stop...He shouted, "Where is he? Where is Paul?"

Paul came out with a pistol in his hand. "Stand back, father," Paul said. "I've done a despicable thing. It's only right that we shall duel. May God have mercy on my soul."

"No, Paul," his father said, "you can't do this. You're an accurate marksman. You'll kill Albert."

Paul pushed him away. "Be my second," he said in a stern voice.

His father nodded, I will.

All agreed on the rules – ten steps back, turn, fire...

When it was over... one man laid on the ground, the other rode off leaving the dust behind him.

Aunt Irene arrived...she saw the men standing around a body...she pushed her way through...

Then she dropped to her knees. "Albert?" she cried in anguish. She then cradled his head in her lap, rocking to-and-fro.

She wept...

She pleaded..."Please, someone, summon a doctor!"

When the doctor arrived, he hurried over to see the injured man; he looked ghastly, the doctor thought he was dead. Albert...laid bleeding profusely.

The doctor split open Albert's coat. He yelled out, "He's alive. It's just a flesh wound to his shoulder; he'll be all right. I'll bandage him up, he'll be fine." Then he added, "He's a real lucky guy..."

Auntie Irene kissed my uncle a million times, saying, "Thank you, God, for saving my husband."

Paul's father said, "It looks like my Paul was the one wanting to be shot! Please forgive my son, Irene."

Then taking Albert's hand and pressing it, said, "I'm sorry, Albert, my son is all mixed up, please forgive him."

He then ordered a wagon to take them back home.

When they reached home, my uncle was carried into the parlor; they laid him down on the divan near the fireplace.

He opened his eyes and said, "Amelia, I did it for you, for your honor," then he fell back to unconsciousness.

I covered him and kissed him and said in a loving whisper, "Thank you, father."

When morning broke, we talked. My uncle said, "We both need time to heal, and when that happens, we will get away for a while. How does that sound to you, Amelia?"

Ellen's eyes widened, she perked up to listen.

"Yes, you too, Ellen," her father said. "We'll all go."

The flesh wound healed and my ordeal subsided.

It was now off to our new adventure. Plans were made for our extensive travel. There was no time set to return.

We traveled on the Danube River. On our route we stopped at Wien (Vienna), Austria. They say that's the crossroads of Europe.

My uncle told us of the Holy Roman and Hapsburg Empires – also of the most beautiful Renaissance, the buildings were of baroque and rococo.

In Vienna we stopped at places where the great musicians lived, like Mozart, Ludwig, Schubert, Brahams, and Strauss. I never knew a world like this existed. The city almost breathes music.

We stopped at the 12th century Cistercian Abbey of Heiligentruz.

Ellen and I were told many times that our mouths were constantly opened in awe.

Right on the Danube is a town called Ulm in Germany. We stayed there for two days and saw the 14th Century Gothic Cathedral. It was the tallest church steeple in the country, 528 feet – that's tall! It had numerous sculptures with colorful stained-glass windows. It also had a museum that dated back to the Middle Ages. It dealt with art and culture in that period of history. I went from room to room, saying "Unbelievable!" No one could catch up to me. I was so fascinated.

What really captivated me was the history of bread and baking. I thought to myself, my dear mama, Mariska, would have loved this. Is this where her secrets came from?

It made a great impression on me. I won't forget it.

We started out again sailing on the river. Then at the head of the Danube was Donaueschingen, Germany.

We stayed at an old inn there. In the morning we traveled the Danube again. That alone was magnificent...

It was now time to start back after many weeks of traveling. We decided to stop only at the spots that interested us before, like Sigmaringen, Germany, and the Schloss Palace.

The Schloss Palace was very imposing, standing on a high rock above the upper Danube Valley.

Then, the Renaissance Palace that was constructed on the site of an older castle in the 16th century...what a beauty...

Then we stopped at Regensburg, Germany, and went back to see the 12th century stone bridge, it extended 985 feet across the Danube; it was so huge!

We passed by the Bavarian Forest to Passau, Germany, where people came aboard bound for Vienna.

Some had their instruments with them, so we had music along the way to Vienna.

But before that we stopped at Linz, Austria. We visited St. Martins Church. St. Martins Church was reconstructed in the seventh century and was the oldest church in Austria.

After our wonderful time at Linz, we reached Vienna. We had sing-alongs and the people danced their hearts out.

Why does this have to end, I thought to myself? It reminded me of when my family was living. We had this kind of fun. How I wish they were here with me now.

Snapping back to reality, I realized that we were on our way to Budapest, Hungary...back home to Miskolc...

We arrived home on a cloudy day. The overcast silhouetted the vineyard with the many grapevines. The scent and scenery...brought back a sentimental nostalgic memory of a loving past. It was good to be back.

All the points of interest we had seen didn't compare to being home. To the left of me I saw the Mátra Mountains. More beautiful than any other mountains I had just seen.

"Miskolc..." I thought to myself out loud.

"What is it?" Auntie asked.

"Look...! We didn't have to leave here to see beauty. I never grasped this splendor before, how could I have missed it?"

"Amelia? Every country has it's own beauty. Seeing other places makes you appreciate what you have. Life is like that, Amelia.

"Some day we'll go to Diosgyor and see the site of the Castle of the 'Queens of Hungary.' Also, Amelia, the Aggtelek Cave, it's one of the largest caverns in Hungary."

"You see, Auntie! I guess that's what it's all about. Making new memories. And I did! I had a wonderful time. Thank you for my lesson in humility."

When we came close to the villa, we saw a horse tied to the post.

Uncle questioned who it was because he didn't recognize the horse.

As the houseman took our carriage, the front door opened wide. I saw someone standing there.

My heart leaped, for I knew it was my Joseph. He looked so handsome in his uniform. There was a cane in his hand! When he approached me, he had a lame movement in his walk. Tears came rushing down my cheeks.

"Amelia?" he shouted. "I came back to you, just like I promised."

"Darling, Joseph! You're hurt!"

"No," he laughed, "it's just a scratch. I'm all right." He put his arms around me and held me so tight.

"Your hair," he said. "I remember its scent of flowers. And...your beautiful face." Then he cupped my face in his hands and he smiled. "Just like I remembered...

"You kept me going, Amelia, I love you." He stood up straight and looked at me. "Will you be my wife, please?"

"Yes," popped out of my mouth without me realizing. "I want to be your wife, that's all I dreamed about."

We spent half the night talking and making plans. Joseph told me that he and his family had purchased a small vineyard in the town of Eger. He was excited when he told me about the town, and what he wanted to do. "I want to grow the finest Tokay grapes in the world and ferment them into an aromatic wine." Without taking a breath he said, "I want to breed horses just like your papa did, and raise sheep," he sounded so eager and full of life.

He could not stop talking, it was as if he had held that in his mind for such a long time, and it finally had to come out.

"Amelia, we'll build our home in the Rocky Bükk Mountains. I can't wait for us to be together," he said.

"They have a county library! I know how you love to read. I'll make sure that we have a chapel for us too. And...we'll have lots of babies." He said that with a big grin from ear to ear. Of course that made me blush.

We kissed...then I felt his hot sweating hand sliding up my dress.

I quickly pushed him away! And just as quickly slapped his face. I almost knocked him off the divan. He stood up and turned from me, rubbing his face.

47

"I'm not that kind of girl! Didn't you know that?"

"Yes," he said. "I also thought you were just a butterfly," he started to laugh, "now I know you're a honey bee, with quite a sting. I'm sorry, my love, that won't happen again."

I saw the print of my hand on his face. I touched it and said, "Joseph, I'm a virgin and will remain so until I marry. I'm sorry, but I had to do that…"

Joseph held my hand, "For a little woman, you're quite strong, that's good…I could use you in the vineyards," he said laughing and kissing my hand.

Then he continued as if nothing had happened. "And…we won't be far from Miskolc."

"We won't?" I said in a breathless tone.

"You'll be able to visit your family often," he said, and kissed me hard. I was in heaven.

The night was creeping in, time for Joseph to leave.

Auntie came into the parlor, and said, "It's late, Joseph, you're welcome to stay in the guest room, if you like."

"Thank you, auntie," he said and bowed. He kissed me goodnight, turned, and said, "See you in the morning, my little honey bee," and winked at me. My heart leaped.

Auntie stayed with me awhile, saying, "This looks serious Amelia."

I then told her of our plans.

She was happy for me, yet sad. "It will be a lonesome house without you," she said. A cluster of tears amassed in her eyes.

"We won't be far from you," I said. "We'll be in Eger. So dry your eyes, dear auntie, be happy for me."

"Amelia? It's time to talk about your dowry. Your parents left you a wealthy woman. The house, land and animals were sold, and the funds kept for you until you marry. Does Joseph know how much you have?"

Not answering her question, I said, "Joseph will provide, he's very independent and very self-reliant. I don't want to take any of that away from him. So until he needs my help, say nothing, please! You hold it for me...will you?"

She kissed my forehead and said, "If that is what you wish, Amelia, say no more."

That night I dreamed of my wedding day...

Chapter 5

Joseph and Amelia Marry

To me, January was the most brutal month of the year. It seems colder, and snows more than any other month.

There were gray skies and great flakes of snow falling...but this time it was different...

It was a fairy tale come true – January 2, 1898, our wedding day, a perfect day; nothing could mar it.

I made my wedding gown, and my aunt gave me her wedding veil to wear – and a satin slip that was my mama's.

Joseph gave me a tiny bouquet of violets from my uncle's hot house, and flowers filled the chapel too. In my bouquet was a ribbon with a little gold locket tied to it. "This was my mother's," Joseph told me later.

A small reception dinner was given. The family and a small group of friends were there.

This was the first time I met Joseph's family. They were as nice and friendly as I dreamed they would be. They talked about the land they all contributed to, and the home they built before the first snow fell.

I was so excited about my life with Joseph. We danced and sang and waited for auntie to call us to her fabulous dinner table. Auntie did all the cooking; she took pride in the culinary art she possessed. She made Paprikas Chicken with noodles – a side dish of vegetables, the works!

I must not forget her bread (the same way my mama baked it) and her churned butter – hot brewed coffee (we usually drank tea). Our toast was made with my uncle's famous Hungarian champagne.

After dinner we danced again. Music filled the room and my heart.

A toast to our happiness was made. "May this joyous union be blessed with lots of loving children." I blushed as we kissed them all and bid them goodnight.

Joseph and I went off to our room. When we came to our door, Joseph picked me up and carried me in. He put me down and kissed me passionately, saying, "We'll do this again in our own home." I was shaking, and I excused myself and went into the dressing room.

Being very shy, I dilly-dallied in putting on my wedding nightgown. Careful not to put it on backwards, I was embarrassed...demure...modest...and self-conscious. He'll think I'm a child? And I'm not! Now I'm a married woman who wants to be with my husband. I must pull myself together!

I finally emerged from the dressing room...there was Joseph sitting on the bed with two glasses of champagne in his hands with that grin on his adorable face.

When I saw him...my gratitude to God immediately came to mind. He had answered my prayers. Joseph had returned to me safe and sound.

With that in mind, I ran over to him almost knocking the glasses out of his hands, he instantly stood up and placed the glasses on the dresser. "My...you're anxious, my little honey bee." (Oh! I wish he had not said that, it made me feel cheap).

He took me into his arms and amorously kissed me. He carried me over to the bed and gently put me down.

It was then I knew I would surrender.

He was patient and tender and very understanding. I won't go into details, but I will say it was a blissful wedding night.

I never knew what the meaning of ecstasy was until then. I was almost delirious with rapture, carried to a place I had never known existed.

We talked, we kissed, and we loved each other all through the night.

He revealed himself and all of his dreams. Disclosing all his fears and the evils of temptation that plagued him.

"Amelia, now that I have you...life will be worth living, I have no fear of anything or anyone," he said.

In the morning we awoke to a clear sky with a winter sun. The joy I felt last night intensified when we kissed each other good-morning.

We stayed in each other's arms, loving each other, seeming not to get enough of one another.

We finally made it downstairs to breakfast. There on the table was my bouquet of violets in a lovely vase. The table was set for two.

The servant came in with breakfast and placed a small feast before us. Sausages and bacon...hot coffee with whipped cream and rolls and assorted pastries. But...I loved the bread the best.

After we nibbled a little and stopped gazing at each other, Joseph inquired where everyone was.

We went into the sitting room, "No one here," he said. He looked out of the window and saw his brothers and sister leaving; they were waving goodbye to my family.

Coming back into the house, Ellen saw us and giggled "Enjoy your breakfast?"

"Pay no attention to her," auntie said. "Come, grab your coats and come with me."

They took us around the eastside of the villa. A black-lacquered sleigh with two black beauty horses with silver tackles on them was standing there. An ancient fur lined blanket for our laps was on the seat with a large basket on top of it.

Auntie said, "This is our wedding gift to both of you."

"Oh, auntie," I replied, "how can I thank you for giving us so much." Hugging them, I said, "I love you all."

Auntie kissed me, saying, "You best get going, it's getting late."

We left them all standing in the hallway while Joseph and I made our way down to the chapel. The chapel...where I asked the Mother of God to protect my Joseph and send him back to me safe and sound. Now was the time to say, "Thank you."

We both knelt in silent prayer with grateful hearts as we gave our thanks.

Then we heard the sleigh being brought around to the front door. It was time to leave.

It was hard saying our good-byes to my adoptive family. Uncle said, "Never say good-bye! Say I'll see ya."

It was sad, yet I was so happy. This was right for us.

Joseph took me to my family burial plot. I laid a flower on each grave (the flowers came from my wedding bouquet of violets). I lingered there, not wanting to leave.

Joseph squeezed my hand and said, "Amelia, we'll be back."

We had planned to stay with Joseph's sister, Julia, but instead Joseph made other arrangements.

"Your aunt gave us a basket of food for our trip to Budapest."

"Budapest?"...I shouted with joy.

"Budapest, here we come," he said. The horses dashed off as he cracked the whip in the air.

"It's our honeymoon, dear heart," he said. "I'll show you where I used to live and where your papa lived also."

The crunch of the snow, the cozy warmth of the fur blanket, gave me a feeling of security. I felt like Juliet and he was my Romeo; I was in love.

We sang and laughter rang out to a cold winter world, by-passing Eger on our way to Budapest.

The jingle of the sleigh...the smell of fresh cold air, and the sight of small animals I had never seen before, was happy for us too.

Will all my days be like this one? "Oh, please God, let it be," I prayed.

Budapest was a modern city with first class hotels. The one we stayed in had a very large plate glass window. From a distance we could see the electric tram cars.

The only time I saw Budapest was from a tour boat on the Danube River trip last year. What a thrilling beautiful city.

We rode on Europe's oldest subway (the one my papa spoke of) which runs between Vorosmarty Square in the Inner City, and City Park, also a scenic trip on a ski lift that climbs to the highest point of Buda's wooded hills. There we donned ski's and...down the slippery trail slope we descended.

We stopped to look at the crystalline river where Joseph pointed to some boys. "They're taking a risk to walk from Buda to the Pest side. I know; I did it! I guess they're adventurous too. Must be great to be that young and foolish. But I'm glad I'm not a boy again."

Then he looked into my eyes and said, "I wouldn't trade anything for my moments with you," and kissed my half-frozen nose. We put up our ski's and rode the tram down.

Joseph took me to where my papa once lived as a boy, Andrassy Avenue. I felt close to my papa, walking down the same avenue he did, and seeing the finished electric subway.

I saw the Budapest Opera House and the Royal staircase and gallery. It was beautiful. Joseph said, "I know you've never seen an opera and we'll come back, I promise!" Then we went to a well-known coffeehouse opposite the opera house for the best coffee I ever tasted.

We saw a castle built in the 13th century by King Bela IV, it was destroyed and rebuilt several times over. It had a library and printing press and innumerable works of art. It was magnificent!

We started back to Eger to begin our new life.

Eger is in a wine-growing and orchard region, a town east on Egar River and Rocky Bükk Mountains.

Joseph said, "Eger is called the 'Rome of Hungry' for its many churches.

"I love it here and so will you, Amelia."

Settling in Eger was exciting. Joseph and his brothers built a stone house with a red tile roof, with double windows and a flower box for my geraniums.

"That's our love flower," Joseph said. "Its heart shaped leaves, its cluster of red and white flowers, were cultivated just for you."

My uncle brought over some of my parents' belongings, and papa's sitting chair that I loved so much, with all its memories. I remember my brother and I sitting on each side of papa. There he would read to us, and say, "Read my children, and you can travel in your mind."

Many of the things auntie gave us I cherished as a youth, bedspreads my mama Mariska had made, dishes belonging to my grandmother Caroline (mama's side).

My aunt gave us her copy of a large painting of Michale Munkacsy's "Christ before Pilate." (I hung that painting in my new little chapel.) He was a famous Hungarian painter born in 1844, died in 1900. He became an instant success with "The last Night of a Condemned Prisoner."

A room was set aside for all my many books, some from Sister Mary who taught me Latin, German and Italian. She said, "Some day it may come in handy."

There was a controversy in the Hungarian schools. The Magyar language was in a struggle. The talk was about Magyarization, teaching Magyar and no other language.

We had so many different cultures, Germans, Slovaks, Romanians, Polish and Yiddish speaking Jews. They came from Russia, Turkey, and all over Europe. Some even came from as far as Japan.

The Hungarian people were up in arms officials claimed, because the children were being confused with all the different languages they had to learn.

Anyway, I loved all languages and wish I could speak in every tongue. I believe communicating is a valuable key to understanding. Although English was very hard for me, I kept at it; with perseverance and the help of Latin, it became easier.

My days became filled with household chores, taking care of my beautiful home, and making sure Joseph was happy.

Sometimes I would go out into the vineyard and bring lunch to my hungry boys (Joseph and his brothers).

Julia, my sister-in-law, was very quiet. She was always telling me that I dressed like I belong to a rich class society. I knew that she didn't like me because I took her brother from her (her hints told me that).

Joseph knew how she felt, but kept making excuses for her, saying, "She took the place of my mother. After the tragic ending of our family, we had a rough time of it," he said. "We didn't have rich relatives to go to, like you. Maybe she resents that? Give her time, she'll learn to like you. Amelia, try to understand and be nice to her."

He left me with my mouth opened. He doesn't have any perception on how his sister's mind works.

I am nice to her; it's Julia who has the problem!

With a lot of effort I tried to get Julia to like me. For awhile I had thought I had succeeded until I learned how she squashed the romance between Ellen and James. They were at the stage of holding hands and looking into each other's eyes, it lasted for about a month. But Julia was still up to her old tricks and she was the cause of their break up.

I took Julia over to Auntie's villa often, trying to get her to like my side of the family.

Then one day she informed me that she was not at all impressed with all the finery she saw. And that our trappings were a show of travesty. We should be ashamed of ourselves for such a display of wealth.

After her envious remarks, I stopped taking her there.

Never confronting her was probably a big mistake!

One day I sent for some material to make a dress for Julia, I was trying to get on her good side. Maybe if she had nicer dresses she would not be so resentful.

Along with that order of material, I sent for some black silk stockings for me. Well, I never heard the end of it. She thought it was shameless of me, and told Joseph to keep an eye on me and the gentlemen friends he has.

I tried to stay out of her way after that. I sewed, cooked and cleaned...read and studied...kept myself busy.

I had a wonderful husband...a beautiful home...and a wonderful family (who came to dinner almost every night).

Julia stayed in her own home and kept to herself.

Chapter 6

Starting a Family

Our first child was born in 1899; Joseph was thrilled he had a son. We named him Joseph John, nicknamed J.J. He had lots of black hair and big brown eyes. He looked more like my side of the family, something like my papa.

Margaret, our next child, came in 1900. Some said, "She was so beautiful, too beautiful to live."

She died at the age of one. It was a crushing blow for all of us. We loved and missed her so much. It left a hole in our hearts never to be filled with anyone but her.

Then, as God willed, He blessed us with another child. On a beautiful sunny August morning...the window was opened to let a fresh breeze come in...and with the breeze came a beautiful white dove...it flew in and perched on my bedpost the moment I had delivered a beautiful little girl.

As I held my beautiful baby, the doctor turned pale and was amazed at the appearance of the dove. He said, "It was a sign from God, this child must be blessed."

"Let's name her Margaret," Joseph said. "She is like our little angel we lost...it will ease our pain a little."

So we did. And he was right.

My Margaret Ann had coal-black hair and deep blue eyes just like her papa. We loved her a great deal, and she was special in many ways. She was our living angel.

Joseph loved being a father, and doted over his children. And I didn't leave my precious ones out of my sight. I made a baby pouch to carry Margaret with me everywhere I went.

So much happened that year of 1903. A recruitment bill for the Austria-Hungarian Army was being talked about. The recruitment would be to maintain the country's status as a great power, a sort of show of arms to the Nations around us. Many men were to be called into service. The people waited anxiously.

There was also a group of military conspirators willing to upset the country, and they finally did when they murdered King Alexander I of Serbia, together with the Queen and many members of the court.

These events scared everyone. "Will war come now?"

The Hungary my parents knew still continued. We had a Dual Monarchy (that began in 1867); it divided the realm of the Hapsburgs into two equal parts called the New Austria-Hungary. Our nation was still torn apart.

There were so many political activists; one didn't know whom to trust. Scuffles in the streets made some fearful to go out.

People tried to ignore the signs. Atheistic propaganda flyers were being passed out; it seemed like it was increasing every day. Joseph called them imbeciles.

The new evil that came into our village was called Communism. Some in the community went to their meetings. They told the villagers they were a "working-class party." Their programs were based on Marxist principles, whose ultimate aim was the establishment of communism in our minds and hearts. God was not a member.

The following year of 1904, there was a renewed strike movement with the discontended workers and the agricultural population. This meant a slow down in our wine production. Our drivers were afraid to cross the strike line to bring our product to the railroad for the market place. The railroads were involved in the slow down also.

The country was nervous because of the conflict between the crown and the coalition. We were threatened by reforms and national resistance. "The smell of war was all around us."

Joseph's older brother joined the army. He said he would go before they recruited him. We will miss him.

The rift between Budapest and the rest of Hungary developed into a sharpening of the conflict between the "Left and Right." Politically and socially the nation was divided. The presence of Socialist Marxist movement was growing.

Then one day Joseph's brother Leslie gave us the bad news that he too was joining the army. He said he would get a better post now, then if he waited for them to call him up. It was a devastating time for all.

Soon James would go, then maybe Joseph. Only through prayer could I cope.

One night James told Joseph that the village was humming about a couple of steamship agents that were looking to book passengers to America. "Let's go talk to them," he said. Joseph agreed.

At the meeting the agent told them that he could get them jobs, in this new country…America…

He also told them that American companies were looking for "Contract Labor" (he didn't tell them that this was outlawed in 1885).

The agent told them, "Not to tell anyone on the ship that they had a job...when asked, just say no, but you would look for one. That way you won't get into trouble."

The agent also said, "I double promise you wealth and freedom. The streets are paved with Gold..."

Not only was his tongue sharp, but the clothes he wore were too. His tailored suit made him look dapper and prosperous. He said he was a returned immigrant, and he had traveled from village to village to speak to his old friends.

He was peddling tickets for $10 to $15 dollars (ordinarily it was $30.00) that would be steerage fare. He said, "This is a special rate the steamship lines were running. Better get them quickly before the rates change."

Some villagers walked out of the meeting. They were told about the steerage passengers from the families that traveled that way. It was known that they were treated much more like cargo than people. But some did not believe that.

Steerage passengers were crammed tightly into ill-ventilated quarters below the water line, or near the shaft where you could feel every vibration. People still doubted.

Many said that at the near ending of the journey, it left them in a state of confusion and frustration. Still this did not curtail their plans to leave.

But this was not for Joseph or James, so they too left the meeting.

Joseph told me everything; his face was drawn. Outside of the meeting hall he said they overheard the angry man saying, "What the agent didn't tell everyone was that we would have to endure deplorable conditions."

Another man chimed in, tears in his eyes, "And the ocean voyage to America was long, strenuous, and a dangerous risk. I had friends that perished."

Joseph continued, visibly moved, "They spoke about the fatality rate that was not uncommon. Many who began the journey never finished it. I'm telling you, Amelia, they gave James and I a lot to think about.

"It's getting dangerous here," Joseph said. "I know if we had to make that trip, we would not go that way. It would be first class or nothing."

Joseph looked frightened... I kept quiet.

That night when all the children were tucked in bed and just the sound of the crackling fire could be heard, Joseph came to me with outstretched arms. We embraced.

This was going to be a romantic evening, I thought to myself.

Instead, in a whispered tone, he said, "Amelia, we must make plans to leave the country." Saying that he rose to his feet, pacing back and forth. He spoke about the meeting, excited and mumbling. He asked me if my uncle would help him get a ticket to board a ship to America!

"Do you think he will help us? I would go first, then you and the children would come after me. Do you think he will get me a ticket... first class, do you? Don't look at me like that!" he said in an angry way. "Will he?"

"Joseph," I said. "Get a hold of yourself. What about the vineyard, our home? What will you do in this new country? Joseph, think! How will you make a living?"

His eyes became tiny; they had a squint to them. He answered me coldly, "I don't know. But I do know this, you must trust in me, believe in me. When I get established, I'll send for you and the children."

Then his face softened. "Remember you told us to
say, 'Jesus, I love you.' Then everything will be all right.
Do you believe that? Or were you just talking?"

"Yes, I do believe in that prayer!" I answered. "But
God wants us to use our common sense too."

He sat down and held my hand. "Listen to me,
Amelia, I'll make sure you travel the safest way, you will
have privileges. You won't have to go to Ellis Island, you
know they call that the 'Island of Tears.' You'll dock in
Hoboken or Jersey City. There's no inspection, and you'll
be able to disembark onto a pier. And... I'll be there!"

He paced the floor... "Customs will clear your
passport and baggage. You won't have to go through any
questioning, or a physical examination when you travel that
way. And I'll be there... How many times do I have to tell
you that!"

He sat next to me and held my hand, saying, "You
and the children will be segregated from the steerage
passengers that's important to me, Amelia."

That made me angry and sad, so I said, "There
should be a law against treating people like animals just
because they can't pay for a first class cabin. It's unfair, and
it's not Christian like."

Joseph stood up. "Amelia," he shouted at me, in a
very mean voice. "There you go again, thinking about
someone else. Let's think about ourselves for a change."

He raised his voice again and was fidgeting. "I want
to leave here, I don't want to go to war again! Don't you
understand?" He stormed out of the room just so he
wouldn't have to say another word to me.

Moments later Joseph came back into the room. He
walked over to me and grabbed me by my arms. He looked
me straight in the eyes. Almost shaking me gently, he said,

"I love you, Amelia, and the children, but if you won't go... I'll go without you. Don't make me choose."

I could feel his nails digging into my arms. "Joseph," I started to cry, "you're too excited, you're hurting me."

He dropped his arms to his side, saying, "Forgive me, I'm sorry. I don't ever want to hurt you... You will just have to understand me. Please understand me."

He kissed me and left.

A couple of days passed, but each day I thought of nothing else but of leaving my home, country and family. The very thought chilled my bones. I remembered my papa and how he said, "I must leave this country I love and take my family to a safer place." This is what my papa would have done; now I know how my mama felt. So I guess this is what we must do.

Just as I was thinking of this, Joseph came in the room. He looked excited. "I spoke to your uncle and he will help us." His face was bright and...he was smiling.

"Here's the plan, Amelia. We have eleven months to shore things up. I will leave first." (He didn't take a breath, but continued). "James will go with me, but before all that happens I must sell everything. Everything must go. I'll find a place in America to live and get a good job. America has beautiful farmlands. I'll find something, you'll see."

Joseph mellowed and said, "I know I didn't ask you, Amelia, I told you! But that's the way it has to be. I'm the man in the family and I make all the decisions. No matter how you feel now, you will thank me later."

I was very heavyhearted to think that he held those beliefs. I was taught that a family decision should be made with the family, that we are a family circle, with our feelings put in the middle of that circle. In that way everyone could have a voice and make a decision with one mind and one spirit!

I didn't tell him that I had agreed before he ordered me to...nor will I ever tell him.

The next day my uncle found out all the particulars of how Joseph was going to leave. First he would put him in touch with the right sources. Although my uncle abandoned the lifestyle of a noble landowner, he still had connections at the capital, so information and papers came fast.

When Joseph and I discussed all the details, we just looked at each other, our eyes wide and teary.

Joseph drew me close to him and said, "This is a bold and daring move – let's not be afraid to take that final step. This is the only way we can stay together as a family. We must make it work."

He fell to his knees and started to cry. "I love this country. I love its people, but our government has let us down and betrayed us."

I have never seen him cry so hard, it came from the depth of his soul. He broke my heart, I cried too....

That night Joseph fell asleep in my arms. As I held him, I thought to myself, "Tomorrow I will have to tell you my secret, dear God help me."

The sun had just come over the horizon and Joseph opened his eyes and smiled at me.

I knew that smile would disappear when I revealed my long awaited secret.

He noticed how serious I was. "What's wrong, Amelia? You look troubled!"

"Nothing is wrong, Joseph! You would have found out soon enough. But...it's just that I was afraid to tell you."

"Tell me what, woman!" he started to raise his voice.

"Joseph," I said quickly, "I'm in the family way again, almost three months now."

"Why didn't you tell me? Is this some sort of trick to make me stay?" Then he laughed. "Do you think this changes anything? It changes nothing!"

He jumped up out of bed, saying, "We'll just have to work harder and faster. I'll be leaving as soon as the baby is born."

When he left the room, I fell on the bed and sobbed, "Oh, papa, papa pray for me. I'm so confused."

Our son Leslie (named after his uncle) was born in 1905. Leslie was not a strong baby, and I worried about him most of the time. How adorable he was, his smile, the way he would look at me...just melted my heart. What a joy he was to me. "Thank you, Lord."

Joseph hardly played with his new son, claiming he had a lot of things to do for the trip.

I was hurt and angry at the same time. I had things to do also. No leisure time for me, yet I made time for my children. Good parents do that!

I prayed to Jesus that he would be a better father, like he was to his other children. I guess he thought Leslie would be in the way.

One morning I heard a lot of cooing coming from Leslie's room. I found Joseph kissing and talking to his little son. He told him that he loved him and was going to make a better world for him. I tiptoed away from the room, thanking God for such an amazing turn-around.

Joseph became fascinated with his new son, so much so that he almost neglected his other children.

Then the time finally came; the papers needed for Joseph's trip arrived. A birth certificate and information that the state officials needed to obtain a passport.

Certain papers had to be prepared before leaving the country. Joseph was ecstatic! But now he would not have time to sell everything, so... I was given the task.

Next, he went to the American Consular Office to obtain a United States Visa.

The booking was made...Joseph will have to take a train to the port – it will be a long trip. So we will have to say our good-bye's here at home.

Joseph had tears in his eyes when the papers arrived. He was told that at the pre-sailing, he may have to wait at the port because train schedules were not linked with the sailing dates.

The night before Joseph left, we loved each other like we never did before. It was sad but sweet, tender but animal like.

It was good-bye till God knows when. I never felt so lonely and yet so loved. We passed the night talking, wrapped in each other's souls.

Joseph awoke early that morning. Everyone did.

It was a quiet morning. No one hardly spoke. J.J. and Margaret stayed right by their papa's side. Margaret asked papa why he had to leave them. J.J. cuddled Margaret saying, "Papa is going to America to make a home for us. We'll see him soon. Right, Papa?"

Joseph was holding Leslie and affectionately kissed him and laid him in his crib. He picked up Margaret and kissed her. Then patting J.J. on the head, said, "You're the man in the house now," he bent down and kissed him.

Joseph drew me close to himself and kissed my lips so hard that I felt a hot sting. "See ya, my love," he whispered.

With a wave good-bye, he said, "Remember papa loves you all."

Julia was there…tears were streaming down her face. She looked at me with contempt. "It's all your fault he's leaving. You wanted so much more out of life than he could give you.

"Joseph talked me into leaving with you and the children. He said I would have a better life there. He didn't want to leave me here alone. I have a good life here. I'm happy here; this is where my roots are.

"Joseph compared me to you! 'Look at your hands, Julia,' he said, 'is this the hands of a lady of the house? Your hands should look like Amelia's. You can find yourself a rich husband in this new country.'"

Now she was becoming hysterical. "I don't have to marry anyone. But I did make him a promise to help you and the children. So I'll go because I love my brother, but I hate you! You broke up my family." With those words, she slapped me hard across the face and left.

J.J. hung onto my skirt and Margaret wanted to climb up to my face. They both started to cry.

"Hush, my sweet ones," I said. "Aunt Julia is upset, everything will be all right."

In my heart I felt very different. How could she treat me this way? I did nothing to her!

Chapter 7

Leaving for America

One week passed, and most of our things were packed. We were getting ready to move into auntie's villa.

My uncle said he had a buyer for our land and beautiful home. It seemed everything was moving so fast, I didn't have time to think.

Julia said she would stay in her home until the last minute. She was not too cooperative, she said she was still struggling with the idea of leaving her country.

On the first day at auntie's villa, I felt a sigh of relief. I was unpacking our belongings, still sorting out in my mind what I would take and what to leave behind.

When all of a sudden, Ellen came storming into the room. She was very upset and angry with me, she said.

"How can you take your children away from their family and country?" she started screaming at me. Then she showed me a newspaper and a magazine publication containing stories about the trip we were about to take.

"Look," she said, shaking my shoulders and shouting. "Look what it says. There are storms that would last for two or three days.

Margaret & J.J. taken at Miskolc, Hungary... Almost two years later they would be in America.

"Read," she went on. "People pray and cry for fear that all humans on board would go down to the bottom of the ocean! Think of your children, Amelia!"

"Ellen," I said, "I am thinking of them. Didn't you listen to Joseph? He said they were fighting in the streets of Moscow, and soon it will be here! Are you not afraid for yourself and your parents? America is a free country; we will be safe there.

"Why don't you all come and start a new life? I read that you don't need a passport to go from one state to another. No armies to invade you! You can live in peace! I want my children to live without fear. So much is happening here. There's too much hatred, they're still fighting over our official language. We have to go.

"The government wants our souls – and – they can't have them. Ellen, they belong to God alone.

"I'm sorry, Ellen – I know you love us and you mean well. We love you! Don't you know my heart aches too?"

Ellen moved close to me (I could feel her breath). She said in a trembling voice, "Will you be able to stand the stench from vomiting people? They have all kinds of sea sickness."

Disgust showed on her face as she went on, "Look," she pressed my hand to an article. "It says you can get mouth rot from their old sharp salty water and food. What will you all eat?

"Amelia, are you willing to let you and your children go through all of this misery?"

She ran over to the crib. "Leslie is just a baby and so is Margaret. What about little J.J.?" She took a deep breath. "You know if anyone of you get sick, they won't accept any of you. It says in this article you will all be deported or quarantined with other sick people."

71

Then Ellen ran over to her mother saying, "Oh my God, this is awful. I can't stand this! Mother, say something to her. Stop her, please stop her!"

Her mother said, "You stop it, Ellen. Joseph assured them they would be safe, otherwise he could not let them go. He said he would let Amelia know what to expect. He wouldn't let them go through what you're saying."

Ellen looked at her mother in an unbelievable way...and left the room in tears...leaving me to ponder what she had said.

I shuddered to think could Ellen be right? Or is it that she just doesn't want us to leave her.

Later that month, our land was sold. Time to bring the furnishings back to auntie's villa.

I gave her back her paintings and my dear papa's chair (that was very heartbreaking for me to do). I could no longer keep all the things I had cherished for years.

I anguished over what I was doing. Was Ellen right? "Dear God, help me! Show me the way."

Julia came over to live with us after her land was sold. She didn't speak much – or smile. I knew how she felt about me, but I let it go. I had too much to do, and I decided I'd let her own hatred consume her.

I received my first letter from Joseph in eight weeks. It was a long letter. I read the letter to everyone (almost everything, some of it was very private, it was just for my eyes and heart only).

Joseph's letter was pitted with a deep concern about us traveling (I almost felt his pain). He said he definitely wanted us to travel in "first class" and not to go any other way – he will send money to pay for it. "Take only first class, Amelia," that was a stern command.

His letter was a little melancholy and sad. He said his brother James found a job with him in a coal mine in Pennsylvania (coal mine country) as a coal breaker. The pay was too low and the work too dirty and unhealthy.

He said, "I'm looking into another job with the Pennsylvania Railroad. The pay would be higher.

"Have faith in me," he said. This was a beautiful country...he loved it, "and you will too, Amelia," he ended with a "kiss to all."

Julia seemed happy to hear from her brother, but was still skeptical.

I read Joseph's letter so many times and even slept with it under my pillow – just to be close to him.

I wrote back to Joseph and told him we had gotten a good price for everything, so he should save his money and put it in a bank. "I will use whatever money I need, and carry the rest to our new home in America." I told him his little son J.J. was now acting like the man of the house, because his papa told him to.

"Baby Leslie is growing stronger, and Margaret is such a great help...she is so sweet and so beautiful, she acts like she is the mother to Leslie. She sings and plays with him all the time. And when she sings, her baby voice is like an angel's...she would dance to make him laugh. I think Margaret is going to be a dancer when she grows up.

"I'm spending most of my time getting ready for our trip. My uncle is preparing me for what is to come, and right now we are waiting for our visas. All I need, Joseph, is the date and the place to meet you. I love you, my love.

"We can't wait to see you and touch your face."

Love forever, Amelia.

Months had gone by, and then we received another letter from Joseph. It was much more cheerful than the last one.

He had found a job in Connecticut with the railroad. He was working as a track-walker. Pretty much the same work he did in Hungary when he was going to school.

James is restless; he misses the vineyards and his homeland.

The letter had good news. Joseph had found an apartment on Johns Street in Hartford (the capital of Connecticut). "It has three bedrooms and a large living room, and a place to take a bath. Please come soon, my love" was how he ended the letter...but not before he gave me the date to leave. My heart was racing – everything will be fine. Now, to roll up my sleeves again. I still have so much to do.

I visited my parents' grave – and shared with them the news. With a sad heart I told them I won't be back to talk to them again...but they will always be in my heart...and some day we will all see each other again. "I love you mama, I love you papa." I left the last flowers I will ever leave there, and threw a kiss to my siblings, then left. Part of my heart was still there. I knew it always would be.

A friend of the family came over to say good-bye. I had known him for years. Bela was his name. He was just a little older than I was and very handsome and single.

Julia made little remarks about him and me. She insinuated we had something going on (she had a wicked mind when it came to me).

My auntie lashed out at her and reassured her that I had scruples. I had to step in and stop a skirmish before it started.

Auntie warned me about her, "Watch your back," she said. "She doesn't like you! Be careful, my little one."

I kept my auntie's words in my mind for the next few days, but forgot about them when our visas and steamship tickets came.

I thought that this would be a happy day – but instead it was a sorrowful one.

My dear uncle was stricken with a heart attack...and died.

The shock was so great, especially for my auntie and Ellen. I saw in a single day how auntie aged in front of my eyes...besides losing us, she now had to face the loss of her dear husband, her love.

The funeral was very large; so many dignitaries were there. The distinguished company said many wonderful things about this great man, the man who was my second father.

Now he too was gone! I had difficulty in understanding why. Why him! Why now!

I prayed for wisdom. But no answer came to me. I felt hopeless and alone once again.

When the funeral was over and my uncle was put to rest, a great calm came over me. Now it was my time to comfort them...just like they did for me, long ago.

Ellen acted very strange when I put my arms around her. She did not make a fuss – she did not shed a tear. She was like stone, she moved like a woman in a spell. I knew how she felt; I left her alone with her thoughts.

I let her grieve in her own way.

It was different with auntie; she let me cry with her. I prayed that God would comfort her in her sorrow.

She reminisced about the "good old days" looking back on her memories, she smiled many times. I knew that God had answered my prayers.

Many days had passed since we buried my dear uncle. Now I had to turn my thoughts back to my long trip.

We had packed two trunks (one small – one large), and four suitcases. I made sure that we had enough food.

Julia said we didn't need food in first class – but I felt we should, just in case.

It was time to leave. Auntie said she would send the rest of our things when we settled.

Oh, how I hated to go at this time. Such sorrow for them to face alone…I put my arms around Ellen and told her I loved her very much. And she was not to worry.

I was smiling at her when I said, "Think of it, Ellen. You and auntie can come visit us when we are all settled in.

"Ellen," I said, "please don't worry about all those things you read about…they were just stories…most of it was not true. Believe me, Joseph would have told me if it were so."

Ellen's facial expression changed from worry to concern, "Do you have enough money? Father said there were no hard rules or laws on how much you must bring with you. Isn't that what father told you, Amelia?"

I answered with a smile, and said, "He told me it would be unsafe to arrive with less than twenty-five dollars each, besides railroad tickets. So don't worry, Joseph will have taken care of everything.

"I didn't forget what you told me, Ellen. I sewed some money into my skirts, and in the children's clothes, just in case we get separated. And yes, I will watch out for thieves." With that I kissed her and felt her love.

Auntie insisted that they accompany us to Fuime (a seaport in northwestern Yugoslavia now known as Rijeka). Fuime was the chief port of Hungary on the Adriatic Sea.

We took a train to the port. When we arrived, we found the ship was late due to the weather, and we had to stay in a private boardinghouse. Some provisions were made for the care of those who had to wait for steamship accommodations.

The Hungarian Government operated and owned the hotel at Fuime (Rijeka). I asked how much it would cost, and they said the steamship companies had to pay for us because they made us wait. It's the law.

Auntie and Ellen could not stay, so we said our good-byes. Ellen grabbed me and whispered, "Until we meet again, dear sister, farewell."

Auntie said, "This will take all my strength to tear myself away from you, my dear child. Write to me as soon as you can, let me know how you are?

"And... about the children, tell them how I loved them." She said, "Please don't forget me." The biggest tears dropped from her eyes.

"Forget you, my dear auntie? I will never ever do that, I love you too much."

J.J. was weeping, and so was Margaret.

They held onto auntie and Ellen so tight. J.J. crying all the time and saying, "I don't want to go! I'll stay here with auntie! You go, mama! I have to take care of auntie... Please let's stay here, let's not go to America...Please?"

"J.J.," I said, "please be a good boy, your papa is waiting for us. He misses us and loves us. Please, J.J. Please? You're upsetting your sister." J.J. stopped and gave me a hug and said, "Mama, don't cry. I don't ever want to see you cry, I'm sorry."

He wiped my tears (as if I was the child) and said, "It's just that I love them so much, mama, and I will miss them."

Auntie and Ellen hugged and kissed us for such a long time, then left, not once looking back...

A great despondent feeling came over me then and stayed with me the rest of the night. Tossing and turning most of the night, I wondered if this was the right move to make. My heart ached.

In the morning I was told the ship had arrived. Our belongings were marked and put down at the dock. It looked like there were thousands of baggage and paraphernalia there. I wondered if we would ever see our baggage again.

After I filled out the manifest (a brief history of incoming aliens), we were told we must have a pre-sailing medical examination. It was then I had found out it would take about fifteen days for the ocean voyage.

We were each given a ticket with a manifest number on it. People were uncertain where to go – what to do next. Some people were very uncivilized, they were vulgar in speech, and you could tell they were uncouth.

My children were nervous and confused. We all were. The people were pushing and shoving so hard that Margaret let go of my hand. She was now lost in the crowd. I screamed her name many times, only to look down at her holding onto my skirt. Tears were streaming down her little face. I quickly picked her up and kissed her. Not a sound came out of her, just those great big tears coming from her deep blue eyes.

As I said, everyone was jumpy, except for the man at the boarding table. He seemed to be the one in charge.

The people who were boarding asked him many questions...and he answered them in their own language.

He must have spoken four or five different languages – even Magyar.

That gentleman took my papers and smiled graciously. He appeared kind and understanding, a likeable person. Then we were pushed along again and I was not given time to ask him any more questions. We were told the ship was to sail soon.

We had to form a line – and then the gangplank was lowered. It seemed that everyone boarded the bridge-like structure at the same time.

Everyone was talking so loud that you couldn't think. No wonder it was hard to observe all the rules they were telling us. The physical pressure exerted on everyone shown on all our faces.

A crewmember looked up our number on his sheet and beckoned us to follow him. He took us down some steep iron steps; we had to hold on tight. J.J. was carrying two suitcases. He let go of one of them – the suitcase burst open when it hit the landing, everything scattered onto the wet floor. He then took us down a dark hallway.

"Where are we going?" I asked, "this doesn't look like first class to me?"

"It's not," he answered.

"But I paid for a first class cabin," I was almost crying. "This is a mistake."

He looked at his sheet and at our numbers, and said, "We have too many people on this ship, the first class cabins are all filled...and so is second class.

"Sorry," he said in an annoyed manner, "you will have to take third class."

My eyes widened and I asked if that was steerage class?

He smiled in a diabolic way, and said, "No! You will have a cabin."

The cabin he showed us had six berths in it. All screwed to the wall (upper and lower). There was very little space to walk. It had a sink in the middle of the room.

I spoke to the crewman in Italian and told him I was not satisfied with the arrangements. And I had pre-paid for first class and that's what I expected – and wanted!

"Can you show me proof?" he said.

"No," I came back rudely. "They took our steamship tickets when we boarded. We paid $85 each, look at my receipt."

He assured me this was the price for third class. "Your luggage will be taken below, signora."...It was as if he didn't hear a word I said. He turned to leave... I pulled on his sleeve. "I want to speak to someone. Take me to the man who spoke to us in Magyar." I described him and said, "He seemed very important, do you know who he is?"

"Oh yes! He's the Foreign Service officer who is a representative for the American Consul."

The crewmember said, "I think his name is Mr. LaGuardia. You better hurry to catch him, we are due to sail pretty soon." He then left in a huff.

I told Julia to stay there with the children – then made my way up the iron stairs...pushed my way through the congested Main Deck and came upon a crew-hand and told him about our inadequate quarters.

He looked at me as if I was crazy...Shaking this very tall man by his two arms, I yelled, "Help me, where can I find the one in charge of the manifest records? Is his name Mr. LaGuardia?"

He frantically pulled himself away from me and was lost in the crowd.

The sailors were yelling to pull the gangway up. They started to pull the big ropes away to free the ship for her to sail.

I cried and screamed down, "Let me speak to Mr. LaGuardia." Then I saw him. He was looking up at me and pointing to me, then to himself. He was saying something? But what?

The noise was so great – I could not hear a word he was saying. I was pushed away from the rail by screaming people waving to their loved ones. The ship was moving. I started to push back, but it was too late...too late!

Chapter 8

Our Voyage

I went back down the slippery steps crying. Now what can I do...?

When I came to the cabin, I dried my eyes. I'll have to pretend to my children and Julia that everything was going to be fine.

Julia looked up at me when I entered the cabin and said, "Can we move upstairs now? We don't even have a door on this cabin. And now we have two more people in this small room." Pointing to the corner berths, she said, "A woman and her son have those beds."

Just then Mrs. Hornack and her son Stephen came in. I introduced myself and turned to Julia and said, "We have to stay here tonight. I'll see what I can do in the morning."

Julia looked at me with her mouth opened; she was in utter confusion. She fixed her berth, jumped in, and pulled the covers over her head.

I was so happy we had someone else in the cabin with us, maybe that's why Julia didn't act up.

I hung up a blanket on the doorway for privacy, then pulled out a small comforter and some clothes and rolled them up to make the pillows softer – the ones they had for us were as hard as stone. The straw that was in the pillows and mattresses were burned after each Atlantic crossing. So

I was told...but I think the ones we had...they forgot to burn. They had an awful odor to them.

We could hardly keep our eyes opened; we were too exhausted to mind the smell.

J.J. slept in the upper berth, Julia and Margaret in the lower one. In spite of the lumpy mattresses and the foul pillows, they fell sound asleep.

Leslie was with me and was unsettled until I breast-fed him, then he went right off to slumberland.

I asked God for His help and Divine Guidance, then I fell asleep.

Before the night was over, I found Margaret had cuddled up to me. She nestled her little head close to my body and was sleeping soundly.

When morning came, I whispered in her ear. "My little one, don't be afraid. Everything will be all right."

I thought to myself I must not let them see me in despair, it would only make matters worse.

I blessed myself and said, "Please, God, help me find the strength to do Your Will. Let me know what to do today. I'm scared."

Margaret and Leslie were still sleeping. I looked for J.J. and he was not in his berth.

A voice from across the room said, "They're all right, Amelia, they went to the toilet. Don't worry, they'll be right back. I told them not to go on deck!"

"Oh, Good God, the deck?" I quickly bounced up from my bed. Just then J.J. came in, the boys were talking and laughing and enjoying each other – they made friends fast.

"J.J.?" I said in an angry tone. "Please do not leave the cabin without telling me."

In an embarrassing low voice, J.J. said, "I'm sorry, mama, but you were sleeping. I'll wake you next time."

I looked at his troubled face and realized he didn't mean to worry me.

"J.J., I too am sorry. I didn't mean to sound so angry. It's just that I worried you may go up on deck without me. Promise you won't do that."

"I promise you, mama, I won't." And...kissed me.

To change the stressful atmosphere, I said, "Are you all hungry?"

No sooner said, the steward came in with some fish and dry bread; some hot tea and milk for the children. I gave them some fruit preserves I brought along with us. And gave some to our new friends. We were all smiles and happy again, except for Julia.

Now to take care of our cabin problems.

After breakfast, Julia look care of the children, and I went to the steward to ask to speak to the captain. He almost laughed in my face. He said the captain is too busy to see me, he had better things to do.

I became very demonstrative... I grabbed his shirt and pulled hard on it. "I want to see the Captain." Then my voice softened... "Please?"

It wasn't long before the Captain came down from the gallery, walking right toward me, a straight stern walk.

The sight of him made my knees buckle out of fear. Now, we were face to face. I finally got up enough nerve to confront him about our cabin.

He had a handsome face and a pleasing demeanor; he patiently listened to my dilemma. He then agreed we had paid too much for a third class phantom cabin.

With a big sigh and moist in his compassionate large brown eyes, he said, "This has happened so many times.

The mercenary steamship companies don't seem to care when they deal with human stock. That's all you are to them."

He looked straight into my eyes and said, "Madam, this will be my last trip to navigate anymore crossings. The barbaric treatment of the steerage passengers is so inhumane that I will not contribute to it any longer."

He then explained that this was the only accommodation left. "I am so sorry, Madam."

The captain promised that he would do everything in his power to make us comfortable. "You may use the Main Dining Room that is used for the first class passengers and whatever else you need (toilet rooms), I will make sure you all get a special pass to enter all of the facilities."

When he walked away, he said, "I'm so sorry." He looked at me once again from a balcony that projected from the ship, then vanished into a silhouette.

When I went back to our cabin, Julia was waiting to hear what had happened. She had dressed the children and once again was packing to leave this cabin.

I told her what the captain said and, with hatred in her eyes, she shouted at me, "It's all your fault."

The children started to cry and J.J. came and put his arms around me – then Elizabeth Hornack and her son Stephen left the cabin.

Julia started to throw things around in her anger. I stepped over and caught her hand. "That's enough of this, let's go up on the deck too. It's a lovely day and things will look better tomorrow."

She stopped and raced off to go on deck by herself. On deck there were people from our village and it was good to see them. They were in steerage and were afraid, but could not get any other accommodations.

Julia, in a perky way, told them, "We have a cabin," and briskly walked away.

One of the villagers lifted his eyes to heaven, saying, "We just wanted to leave Hungary, we were fearful for our lives."

Another said he would "rather lose his life in the ocean, than live under tyranny."

So...steerage or not, they would make the best of it. We walked away feeling very sorry for them and feeling very lucky for ourselves.

Up on deck we had time to think and pray, and feel the saltwater air brush against our skin... Just to breathe air and fill our lungs was a joy. The ocean was a little choppy, and at times we had to hold onto each other. Sometimes the salt water would spray us (Margaret didn't like that, she kept putting her body into my dress to cover her head).

The whistle signal sounded, indicating our time was up. Now the next shift could come up to get some clean ocean air. But instead of going to the cabin, we decided to go to the Main Dining Room. It was so beautiful, what a change from our dreary cabin.

Lovely tablecloths donned the circular tables. The silverware sparkled and the glasses twinkled with flashes of light from the opened portholes.

The waiter fixed two tables together, then we ordered.

The grandeur of it all reminded me of Joseph and I in Budapest on our honeymoon. I sat there trying to hide the tears in my eyes.

We spent a great deal of time at the table just talking and laughing.

Dusk was settling in upon us and the beautiful lights went on in the dining room. We hated to go back downstairs to our dingy room.

I prayed that the moon would shine again so it would not be so pitch black...like the other night...Margaret was so afraid. I begged the Lord this trip would be over soon, if only for her sake.

Elizabeth said she was not feeling well when we were dining. I noticed she picked at her food, and she looked pale. Stephen doted over her as if he were the mother. What a wonderful child he is to her. God had surely blessed her.

By now we were far out from Fiume Seaport where we started.

After sailing the Adriatic Sea, we then made our way to the Ionian Sea. We stopped at Naples, Italy. There we picked up some more passengers – I wondered where they were going to put them all. There must have been hundreds of people.

How can they feed them? Most of them were young adults with children. I asked the steward about them and he said, "They have to fill up the steerage area. It will take at least a thousand passengers or more, besides they should have their own food." I didn't believe him.

We were sailing on the Mediterranean Sea, bypassing Sicily. The Mediterranean was known for its rough sea, but it was unusually calm for us.

We passed through the Straits of Gibraltar (south tip of Spain and north of Morocco). Everyone was getting excited when they found out that the Straits were between Europe and Africa, for that meant we were on our way out to the entrance of the Atlantic Ocean, then on to the "Golden Land, America."

I listened to the stories of why they left their homeland. Each was so different. Some spoke of freedom, some for riches, others for adventure.

America was painted with a different brush for all of them. And I? I wanted my children to have God in their lives. I wanted them to have a meaningful life before they too met their Maker.

The first few days on the Atlantic were uneventful, except for the three couples that just met on the ship and married. People came on deck and brought their musical instruments along with them. We sang and danced. The children were playing and laughing. Even Margaret enjoyed the peace and calm. She started to forget her fears. Once again I saw a happy and smiling face, playing with her brother Leslie. But I had noticed that when she did speak, she stuttered.

Even the first class passengers seemed to be enjoying the pleasantry, although they didn't care to come in contact with us. That was fine, because we ignored them also.

I saw the Captain, he vigorously waved to me, then disappeared. I must admit my heart skipped a beat faster. Good thing Julia was not around.

One day while on deck, the captain came over to me. He greeted me warmly and invited us over to the dining hall. I said yes for all of us, that we would be delighted.

During our meal, we laughed and talked about everything under the sun. I told him all the things that had happened to us. He was very sympathetic to my stories. I then asked him about the Foreign Service Officer, Mr. LaGuardia.

He told me that he knew him very well, and that someday he would become a real important person.

Amelia Everything Will Be All Right

Julia didn't join in the conversation. She only looked at me with disapproving glares. I didn't let that bother me, for I was enjoying the moment. I was delighted with a captivating...charming...sensitive person. At times he was profoundly deep. I was impressed.

Julia, I thought to myself, you are not going to spoil the night with your evil mind.

Sure enough, after he left us, Julia commented on how much attention he had given me. She raised her eyebrow and said, "He must have had some encouragement to be so brazen."

After Julia made her ugly comment, she turned away from me and walked ahead of us.

Elizabeth patted my hand and said, "Don't let her get to you, she seems envious of you and your wonderful personality."

I blushed and said, "Thank you for being kind, people are starving for kindness, it's a rare commodity. Julia could sure learn from you, Elizabeth."

Later in the cabin to keep the peace I didn't scold Julia for her scandalous remarks. Instead I let it go by. If my Joseph heard her, he surely would have been angry.

Everyone fell asleep fast. But, not me. I thought, how could Julia treat me this way? No one has ever spoken to me like that. Why do I permit it? She tears me down in front of everyone, even my children. Maybe I should clobber her mouth. Or throw her overboard. Oh...what am I thinking of...dear God erase these thoughts from my mind. It's not a Christian attitude to take, and Sister Mary would be greatly disappointed in me. So... I prayed. "Dear Sweet Jesus, help me not to feel this way. Help me to understand her and forgive her. And try to love her." I blessed myself and fell asleep.

As the days went by, Stephen and J.J. became very close. Stephen was at least four years older than J.J. But, J.J. was older for his age. Margaret stuck close to me – she didn't play with Leslie like she use to. She was very quiet – no smiles – no songs.

She was a very scared little girl. When the noise from the engine room would get louder, Margaret would cup her ears and scream. My heart was breaking.

The crying and sounds from below disturbed my little girl so much she hardly slept. She didn't want to walk, she wanted me to carry her everywhere.

Julia said I was spoiling her, what she needed was a good spanking.

I was so grateful that Elizabeth would talk sweetly to Margaret. What a blessing Elizabeth had become. She was a pleasant person. I was happy she was in our cabin, especially when Julia acted up – Elizabeth would come to my defense.

The voyage was hard, and the ocean changeable, even the skies looked different.

Some days the sun would shine so brightly, making everything it touched seem so clean. Our ship that needed painting even looked good to me.

There were days when the ocean would be so rough you could hardly stand upright. At times it would be a hazardous undertaking to venture out of the cabin. But it was worth the risk just to look at the angry ocean.

To see the mounts of foam, and the different colors the waves made, was spectacular. The height and depth of the ferocious ocean whitecaps seemed peaceful, yet hostile at the same time. It almost resembled life.

The contradictions and the inconsistencies of the ocean startled the imagination. One would have to see for themselves the majesty, the Power of God.

When we had a small storm, we had to close our porthole hatch (the crew saw to that). The air became stifled...we could smell that awful odor. At times we felt that we would choke and suffocate. Sometimes Margaret would vomit.

Then one night a big awful storm came. The wind could be heard beating against the ship – and the waves lashing all around us – some of the waves covered the entire ship.

There was explosive thundering and fierce lightening we had never heard nor seen before.

The familiar sound we were used to...could just be heard faintly...like the cranking of the engine, the cries of the young ones, and loud voices of family members.

Next, unexpectedly, came an amazing calmness...the engine stopped. Dead silence ensued...you could hear your heart pounding...and just the sounds of the raging ocean.

The loud crackling of lightning in the atmosphere spurt out electrical charges that lit up the once unseen clouds.

We never ever heard sounds like that before. The ship shook. It seemed it would last forever. We all thought that this was the end of us. Everyone was said to be whispering a prayer. "Dear God, help us!"

Then suddenly the engine started up again. The All Powerful Almighty heard our plea and answered our prayers. The storm stopped.

I never thought I would love the sound of the earsplitting engine, and the not so muffled sounds of voices. Now tonight we will all get some needed rest.

The sun came up early the next morning. It was never more welcomed...we were told that we could go up on deck after breakfast...and we did.

I noticed that a few of my villagers were not there. I wondered... and then worried.

That afternoon, when Leslie and Margaret were asleep, I made my way down the iron slippery stairs to the steerage area, out of curiosity and concern.

When I reached the bottom of the stairs, a terrible stench tore at my nostrils. It was so overpowering I could hardly breath...my eyes could not believe the rows of bunks that were in the hundreds...I peered down the low line alley of human beings. I heard different languages all at the same time. How confusing it was.

The floors were just a series of boards, like a flat piece of wood. The ceilings were made up of pipes...

Pipes going everywhere. They went to the length and width of the ship.

I was now below the deck section of the ship. It was where the steerage apparatus was for the vessel.

The passengers were limited to a very tiny space. They were all bunched together without hardly any leg room. The clearance from top to bottom prevented any one of height to stand up. I'm 5 foot 6 inches and I could not stand. I literally was bent over and sometimes had to crawl on my hands and knees over the bunks. Strange! No one seemed to mind me climbing over them.

Then one of the villagers spotted me and yelled, "Amelia, over here!" It was Lucy, she looked awful. She began telling me what had happened during the big storm. How everyone panicked.

"We had no ventilation because all the hatches were fastened down during the storm. Cut off from oxygen, my mother suffocated and died... She had a heart condition. Now I have no one. They quickly fed her to the fishes. Oh, my poor mother."

She held her head, rocking back and forth. "Go!" she said, "you may get sick down here." Then she started to cry. She did not hear my words of comfort. But beckoned for me to leave her. Before I left, I held her hand. "Lucy, say this prayer with me. Jesus, I love you, help me, stay with me, walk with me, touch my heart, heal me!" She repeated the prayer...then I left her side as she cried uncontrollably.

On leaving I saw a man lying in his own feces, not stirring. Others, complaining to each other, why they left their country. "Was it for this?"

I left the deplorable, wretched sight vowing to do something. Somehow! Sometime!... Tell someone.

Characterization of the steerage passengers as outcast people to be shunned to me was a great sin...they needed to be embraced, and loved, and understood. These were not derelicts, vagabonds, or destitute people (in the sense that they had nothing). Not castaways, as they were called, but courageous souls. Like the Iron lady that stands in the harbor speaks of: the downtrodden, people with religious beliefs, principles... law-abiding, hard-working, innocent victims.

How sad to see God's Image, being treated in such a tragic way.

I blessed myself and quietly said, "Jesus, I love your Image, please bless them and keep them safe."

When I reached our cabin, I heard screaming and crying. Entering the cabin, I heard, "It's all your fault, Amelia."

"What's wrong?" I said.

"It's Margaret!" Julie said. "She is missing."

"What? She was sleeping when I left her with you, Julia, you were to watch her."

I felt lifeless as I searched for her everywhere!

Margaret could not be found anywhere! The captain immediately sounded the emergency alarm that a passenger was missing.

The contingency plan I was told was to search the bow (front section of the ship), to stern (rear part of the ship). And...after that!

It was assumed a hand/or passenger was overboard.

I went on deck, calling my little girl's name. "Margaret? Margaret!" I was in a panic. I could hardly stand, and my voice was getting weaker.

I was horrified to think she fell overboard - my little one in that big black ocean.

At one time I went to the edge of the deck, only to be pulled back by a seaman. I was screaming and trying to reach the water. Trying to see if my little girl was swallowed up, submerged in a giant fish's mouth.

The shrieks that came from me were unreal and sounded like an animal caught in a trap.

My lamentations were so great that I passed out. I was brought to my cabin by the captain, he had carried me in his arms, weeping and sobbing. He placed me on my bunk, and hastily left the instructions to Julia.

"Keep your eyes on her at all times, do not let her go up on deck."

It was at the crack of dawn when I was awakened by a slight nudge on my shoulder, and a shaken voice said, "She's safe, Amelia." The captain put her on my breast.

"She is sleeping soundly," he said.

I kissed her all over her tiny face, the tears of joy fell on her, while I checked her from top to bottom.

"Where was she?" I said rejoicing.

The captain answered in a nervous laughter. "Asleep in a row-boat. She must have gotten scared and lost her way, then she climbed into the boat and fell asleep crying. Her hair was bathed in her tears."

When Margaret awoke she cried, "I was looking for you, mama. I asked Baby Jesus to help me find you. And...here you are, dear mama." She smiled and fell asleep in my arms.

I never left her out of my sight since then.

"Thank you, Baby Jesus, for answering Margaret's prayer."

Chapter 9

Ellis Island

Four days later land was spotted. Everyone that was allowed went on deck. We all took turns because of the amount of passengers the ship held.

People were screaming and crying for joy. They were dancing and throwing things up in the air. It was a wonderful sight to see.

Elizabeth felt too sick and weak to come on deck and enjoy the wonderful experience of seeing the Great Lady.

When she heard the news of land sighted, she smiled a broad smile and blessed herself.

She called Stephen over to her side and was whispering to him. Stephen had tears streaming down his face; he could not contain himself.

We did not hear what Elizabeth was saying to him; we could only surmise what was going on.

When his mother fell asleep, Stephen came over to me. He sat down close to me and said, "People are trembling in their shoes at the sight of land and the Great Lady standing there just waiting for us to see her. And…here my sweet mother lies, never to see it." He sunk his head into my breast and sobbed.

I held Stephen while he sobbed and said, "We must trust in God's Wisdom and Plan. We don't know why bad

Ellis Island

Joseph had us stop at the visitor's
portrait stall to take a picture...
     "A Family Picture..."
(left to right) Margaret, me,
Leslie and J.J..
My heart almost broke when Stephen
was not included.
     I was told to "smile" - but
how could I? Not while Stephen
stood there with his face drawn and
in tears - just watching.
     "Can Stephen get into the
picture?" I asked - "No!"
Joseph said in a harsh voice.

things happen to good people. Everything has its reason. We are to only hope and pray that we fit into God's Plans.

"Find strength, Stephen, in knowing that God loves you and your sweet mother. Leave tomorrow's worries for tomorrow."

I kissed him and rocked him, and sang a song he loved. He fell asleep in my arms.

The next day we saw the shadow of Her... "The Great Iron Lady"... There She was, raised high in the sky – with a torch in Her right hand – and those words written on Her tablet were for us...

"Bring me your tired and tempestuous toss. I lift my lamp besides the Golden Shores." She was beautiful, breathtaking, what an awesome figure standing there. I fell in love with Her...

"Thank you, Jesus," I said, "Thank you for such a beautiful Lady to welcome us, and a wonderful country." I could not speak; my heart was so full of love for her.

I said to myself, this is now my new country – I will be a good American, I just know I will.

That night hardly anyone slept, we were too excited.

The engine was not clanging; the ship seemed to be gliding in softly. The cries in the night stopped. All you could hear were whispers.

The ship was not rocking back and forth like it violently did before. It was so peaceful and serene that even Julia was quiet, her face showed a sign of relief.

The quietness gave me time to think. My thoughts were of Joseph – to see his face, and the joy we would share again.

This time my heart was fluttering out of happiness – not out of fear or anxiety. I fell asleep, only to be awakened by the sun creeping into the porthole.

My arms were around Margaret, I was thinking of our long trip from Hungary. I counted on my fingers how many days it took…twenty-one days? It seemed like a life time; long days and much longer nights.

Snapping back from thinking of the hard times, I said no more dwelling on what was, only what will be.

I gathered our belongings together and checked the large sum of money I had in the form of a bank note. Some of the money was from my parents' estate (the sale of our land and home). I was very nervous wondering how to keep it safe from thievery.

I wanted to show the authorities all my assets so we could enter the country without a problem. Rumors had it that some officers in the authorities took money and jewelry from emigrants who did not speak or understand English.

So…thinking it over, I decided to hide the notes and just show the paper money I had sewn in our clothing.

While trying to figure out what to do, I glanced over at Elizabeth; she beckoned to me. When by her side I noticed how sickly she looked. Her face was as white as chalk, her cheeks were red. She told me she was ill, and they may not let her into the country.

"My Stephen," she cried, "they will make him return with me to Hungary. I don't want that. Amelia, I'm very sick. What would my Stephen do? He's only a boy, he's eleven years old. He can't take care of me.

"Amelia, I sold everything to get this far, please promise me that you will care for the boy until I can return. Please say you will be his guardian. I will give you the rest of my money, please?"

She started to shake – her voice rose a bit. I put my finger on her lips. "Shush," I said. "We don't want to wake anyone, Elizabeth. If you can't make it at this time, you will next time. If you have to go back, I will speak to the captain. I'll tell him to move you into a first class cabin. But... Elizabeth, we are going ahead of ourselves, you will be all right. Let God do His job, He knows what's best. Have faith. Don't worry. I'll help you, Elizabeth."

She smiled and released a big sigh, then sank into the bunk bed and closed her eyes.

"Elizabeth? Elizabeth?"... I shook her. She opened her eyes and whispered, "Thank you, Amelia, I knew I could count on you, you're a good woman."

I quickly left her to wash up and get everything ready. I put on my best dress, the one that I had my money sewn into. By that time, everyone was up, and I helped them to get ready for our big day.

"We are all going to look nice for your papa," I said happily. Margaret smiled, but didn't say a word. She had hardly spoken without stuttering the entire trip; I was worried sick about it. She was afraid and stuck by my side constantly.

J.J. put on his new suit. Leslie had on his white skirt and bonnet, the one he was baptized in. I made sure Stephen had washed and dressed, I told him I would care for him like my own. Of course, he did not know what I meant.

We all went upstairs for breakfast. After we ate, Julia stayed with the children in the dining hall while I brought... hot tea to Elizabeth, and some preserves for her bread. But...she could not eat. She drank the tea and started to vomit. She was burning up with a fever.

I summoned the steward to get the captain. He came right away to see her. The captain examined her and quickly evaluated that she was extremely ill. He took me aside and said, "She does not look good. I'm worried."

The captain took my hand and held it tight, saying, "I don't think she will make it into the country."

I asked the captain for a first class cabin for her and he agreed. "That's the least we can do," he said.

Just then Elizabeth called out, "Captain? Amelia said she would take care of my son, Stephen, until I can return, please help me."

The captain's voice cracked as he answered her. "I will help you, I promise, Elizabeth!" He then glanced down at me and gently kissed my cheek. I blushed, but I did not pull away. He said, "I'll put on the manifest that you are Stephen's guardian. I'll stand by you. Everything will be fine, don't worry."

He walked over to Elizabeth, touched her face and said, "If you don't believe in angels, believe now! For Amelia is your angel." He quickly left, after giving me a sympathetic look and a wink in his eye.

Once the ship docked – it was boarded by many immigrant landing inspectors and medical officers who examined the cabin class passengers.

The first and second class passed through quickly. Free to go through customs at the barge office, just like Joseph said. The rest of us waited in turn.

I checked many times to see how Elizabeth was doing. Stephen was unaware of the goings on. He was so wrapped up in the excitement.

I went back upstairs, just in time to see the captain speaking to the boarding inspectors and a medical officer. The medical officer had seen Elizabeth and was reporting to the captain that, "She had to go back to be treated on the other side."

I found out later from the captain that the shipping company was responsible for her – and her free passage back to Hungary. "I pledge to you she will be well taken care of," the captain uttered again.

I hung my head in deep despair, feeling hopelessness like I never felt before. The captain put his arms around me as I cried. When he released me from our embrace, my eyes caught a glimpse of Julia hiding in the shadows.

I paid no attention to her because I thought she would understand when she becomes aware of what has happened. I know she will feel sorry for Elizabeth too.

When I reached the deck, Julia yelled out to me, "Here we are." When I reached them, she gave me a degrading stare. She tightened her teeth together and said, "You could be more discreet with your ship romance."

I could not believe what I had just heard. Even after I told her about Elizabeth, she threatened to tell Joseph all about me and my so-called romance.

I became so angry I couldn't stop from saying, "Tell him what you want, you cold hearted witch."

She laughed at me…like she was the devil's consort, "Don't act like you're an angel," she said.

"You're a ridiculous and sinful woman, Julia. I'll have to pray real hard for you. Do you think Joseph will ever listen to you? He loves and trusts me.

"Enough of this, soon you'll be on your own and good riddance."

Feeling this angry about her, I must confess felt good. Satan was working overtime.

We stood in line silently, with chattering people all around us. By the time the inspection was completed for the whole ship, it was dusk.

We had to stay the night. We were all so fatigued anyway, it was welcomed.

The children fell asleep as soon as their heads hit the straw pillows. Stephen was by his mother's side, holding her hand and crying. His mother was asleep from the medicine they gave her.

I went over and told him what his mother said. Kissing him, I said, "You will stay with us, Stephen – just like your mother wants. She will return and you will be a family again – be strong and trust in God. Remember, Stephen, you have us. And now you have a brother, J.J. – he loves you and looks up to you. Show him how strong you can be, even when your heart is breaking. Stephen, I love you."

We heard loud noises – like guns going off. "Oh, good God, no! There is war here too?" I said.

Then I heard people laughing and yelling something. It woke the children up. They started to cry…I gathered some bedding together and draped it over the children and took them up on deck.

It was so crowded, I didn't know what was happening. The children were so afraid. We were all fearful.

Someone shouted, "God Bless America. This is the 4th of July. It's Independence Day, the day of freedom."

Then I remembered what I had read about… "July 4, 1776." I too laughed and cried. What a beautiful day to come to my new country.

We went back downstairs. I told Julia, "They say tomorrow will be a lot of hassle and some hardship, so let's get some rest."

Her eyes were like steel, the coldness went through me. She nodded and said nothing and went off to bed.

Sure enough, in the morning impetuous people pushed and shoved to get ahead of each other.

The ferryboat ride between Ellis Island and the barge office was every thirty minutes on the hour, and only thirty passengers at a time. They went by manifest numbers and could take all day to accomplish this task, they said.

I prayed to God that was not going to happen.

Today we say our good-byes to Elizabeth...

I gave her Joseph's home address and kissed her and said, "See you soon, my dear lady."

She answered in a weak voice, "Yes, Amelia, yes."

We left Stephen to say farewell to his beloved mother, and we waited upstairs on deck for him.

He came up, face wet with tears – just in time to board the ferryboat. Stephen looked back at the ship as we sailed away, and said, "Good-bye, my sweet mother, till we meet in heaven." Then he sank his face into his hands and cried uncontrollably. So did I!

Aboard the ferry, we were all given landing cards to enter the United States.

In a very short time, we saw Ellis Island at a distance. We were hurried off the ferry to the barge office. Then back on the ferry to Ellis Island. On the left of us, you could see the very tall buildings in the city.

When we reached our destination, we were brought into a very large structure. It looked like a castle to me. We were all grouped together in the Administration building and directed to the Main floor.

On the first floor was the baggage storage and claim area. It looked like there were thousands of people in the baggage area. Trunks, bags, and suitcases covered the entire floor.

People had their sentimental knickknacks and comforters. Children sat on their luggage bags, holding their stuffed dolls and baby pillows. And... some people were sleeping on them. Others were crying and everyone talking at the same time. It was worse than the ship's noise. It was like a mad house! Unbelievable.

We had to leave our belongings there for the duration of the inspection process. I heard that some people lost their luggage. I didn't like that.

They told us we could take the children into a dormitory where nice clean white beds could be used. There was a very clean restaurant that sold soup, sandwiches and milk.

That all sounded good to us... but, instead we were all shuffled off to the registry room on the second floor.

We were told we had to go through two examinations. One medical, the other legal, each would take less than ten minutes.

The stairs were sectioned off with wire for twenty-five to thirty-five people at a time, so we could all stay in line. It was like going through a stockyard and we were the livestock.

Then there were so many stairs to climb. And doctors watched to see if anyone had difficulty with them. Those that couldn't do it were singled out. I understood that they were looking to weed out the lame, and the feeble so that they would not be placed on welfare later.

Doctors were looking for signs that may prevent us from earning a living and checked for communicable, or venereal diseases.

A lot of the doctors were kind, they took into account that we had such a long voyage and were fatigued.

Those that didn't pass were marked on their lapels with chalk and sent to a confinement room and examined closely.

Everyone waited patiently for the physical examination, knowing that in just a few hours they would be free to begin a new life.

If we could endure a crossing on a frightful ocean, we could endure this. I guess that's what kept most of us going.

What I dreaded most was the eye examination. Your upper eyelids were folded back by a silver instrument; it was very painful. Margaret didn't go through that, the doctor took pity on her and let her pass. "Thank you, Jesus."

Then came the legal examination. It was mostly to prove that the information on the ship's manifest was true. Then they had to decide if each immigrant had enough money for a train ticket or temporary quarters.

The emotional experience was something I wouldn't want to repeat. The thought of being rejected crossed all our minds.

The sigh of relief came when the "Identification tag" was put around our neck, as the first sign of our "Americanization."

Friends and relations waited to greet continuous lines of happy faces, who passed all the examinations.

Thank God we all passed, but... barely. Margaret didn't want to walk for the doctors or talk to them. She would not let go of my dress. And she would not let them examine her completely.

Thank God the doctor had a little girl like Margaret. He said he realized she was young and scared.

We hurried to the baggage room – where we left our possessions. We sat on hard benches and listened for our names to be called.

When a sponsoring person arrived, they would go to the information department. There an inspector would go over the manifest with them, making sure the sponsor was the correct person to leave them in their charge.

Soon our name was called. We were rushed to a chicken wire gate.

I looked for Joseph. I searched all the faces.

He was not there...

A tall man, dressed in a beautiful store-bought suit, a fancy cap on his head, and...a mustache that twirled up. And...very shiny shoes with spats.

Was calling my name?

I didn't know who he was. When I had gotten closer to him, he smiled. That smile? I knew that smile...it was my Joseph's.

I quickly gave Margaret to Julia, who was holding Leslie, "What is the matter?" she said. "Are you crazy?"

Ignoring her completely, I ran over to that smiling man. My Joseph...

We kissed each other a thousand times. The tears streaming down my face.

"Is this really you, Joseph?" He kissed me again and I knew it was him...

J.J. walked up to his papa in a shy manner and hugged him. "Is it really you, papa?" he said.

"My... you've grown so tall," papa said, as he mussed his son's hair and kissed him on the forehead.

Margaret was not sure what to do...So when papa picked her up, she looked at me, then at him. I nodded in approval. She then planted a great big kiss on his face and smiled.

Papa kissed Leslie and remarked how pale he looked.

Julia pushed me aside and grabbed her brother and kissed him, saying, "This was a terrible trip. I have a lot to tell you."

Chapter 10

The Loss of Leslie

After Julia had told Joseph about "This terrible trip," I immediately pushed her aside like she did me. "And...because of you, Julia, the 'terrible trip' was worse than it should have been!" I said.

"We'll discuss this later, meanwhile," I said smiling, "Joseph, I would like to introduce you to Stephen." And taking Joseph and Stephen by their hands at the same time, said, "This young boy is coming to live with us for a short time." Joseph looked stunned as they shook hands.

I took Joseph aside and explained very little to him about our new responsibilities. And promised to tell him later.

He warmly smiled and said, "I respect your wishes. Amelia, you can tell me later, my love."

Grabbing my hand and pressing it hard, my Joseph took us to the train station without another word about Stephen, although in doing so, he carried a funny look on his face that I couldn't make out.

He had a basket of food he purchased at the Ellis Island cafeteria while waiting for us.

"Children? This is for our train ride," he said. "You all must be very hungry."

Joseph took off our identification tags that were around our necks and said, "I'll throw this away; it's all behind you now.

"Now! My darling Amelia, to your new home." He kissed me passionately on my dry lips and hugged me tightly as the children looked on.

We boarded the train and Stephen sat alone. He was rigid as he stared out of the window with tears running down his torturous face and looking up to the heavens. I knew… what was going through his mind. I knew… he was feeling the loss of his mother.

I left Margaret playing with her papa's waxed mustache, she was fascinated by it. Joseph was always clean shaven, so I too will have to get use to it.

I snuggled up close to Stephen, my face touching his. "Cry all you want to son, brave men cry too. Jesus cried. Ask Him to help you. Pray for your mother, ask her to help you over these hard times. That's all we can do right now."

Stephen smiled like the angels do. With a kiss and a caress, I said, "Come sit with J.J., your new brother. Have some fun now. Look at all the new things you both can see together. If you have tears in your eyes, you'll miss them."

I went back to sit with Joseph to talk to him about our new life in our new country. I was fascinated with my unfamiliar surroundings. And…unsuspecting about my new looking husband.

Joseph told me very little about his new job he had on a farm outside the city of Hartford. He explained he would come home on the weekends.

Also he wanted to be able to buy a farm like the one he worked on. The way he spoke about this new job made me reluctant to ask him anymore questions.

Lord….I had a million of them.

Anyway, all I wanted to do was to look at him and press his hand in mine.

We sat so close to each other on our way to Connecticut. While soaking in each other's presence, Julia came over and nudged me to get up.

"Amelia! I left Leslie in my seat, go to him! I want to speak to my brother. Besides your baby needs you; I think he's hungry."

When she sat down with her brother, she made Margaret go sit with me.

I watched Julia as she talked to Joseph. Her hands were flying, and at one time he caressed her. At times he looked furious, his face reddened.

What was she saying? Whatever it was, I could see that it affected him deeply.

Thank God the train ride was short. We were in Hartford now. The trees were beautiful, the hot breeze was welcomed.

The train stopped at our station. Joseph gathered our belongings, and James, my brother-in-law was waiting for us with smiles from ear to ear.

We greeted each other with emotional hugs. It was good to see him again. He did put on some weight; he looked great.

We all piled into the buggy, and off we went to our new home.

When we arrived at Johns Street, Joseph said, "This is it. I hope it's all right." The luggage was taken off the buggy. All except Julia's.

Then I was told Julia will be staying with James on the farm where Joseph and James worked.

I didn't say a word. I left it up to Joseph to tell me what was wrong. And...he didn't.

The apartment was small but adequate, far short of the beautiful home we left in Europe. I was grateful Julia was not going to stay with us, but wondered why her plans were changed so suddenly.

Or was it sudden? Did she know about Joseph's new job? I didn't... Did they conspire together? And when? I quickly changed my thoughts. Thinking we're all together now, a family, at last. "Oh thank you, Jesus," my heart sang.

That night fulfilled my longings. I was in my Joseph's arms again. I love him so much; that's all that matters.

I awoke in the middle of the night, it was so very hot. My nightgown was moist and beads of perspiration were on my face. My whole body felt sticky.

I turned to touch Joseph, but he was not there. I saw him sitting at the window with a cigarette in his mouth. I was surprised. I never knew Joseph to smoke.

I got up and went over to him. I touched his shoulders gently, but he quickly stood up. "What are you doing?" he said in an irritated tone.

"Joseph? It's me. What's wrong?"

He grumbled, "Nothing! You startled me," pushing me away he said, "I was just thinking we have to talk. I was thinking about this child, Stephen. How long do we have to keep him? Did his mother give you any money to take care of him? This is an expense we don't need.

"You see, Amelia, we don't have too much room here for ourselves, let alone another person."

I answered with a plea in my voice. "Joseph, he's just a little boy. He doesn't eat much."

I told him it was not like him to take this kind of attitude. "You've changed." (He could see my body stiffening) I said, "Is this what's bothering you? Or is it something else? Tell me. What's wrong? Even as I laid in your arms tonight, there was something missing. Joseph, you know how much I love you. Don't you?"

He looked almost sad, "Yes I do," he answered.

He took my hand and then pushed me back into bed. "It's late. Morning is almost here. I'll have to leave early for work." He kissed me and covered me, got into bed, and went right off to sleep.

I awoke in the early morning hours, only to find Joseph had dressed and eaten breakfast. He came over to kiss me and say, "Rest, dear heart, you have a big day ahead of you. I'll see you in four days. We will talk then...I have to hurry now, bye."

I called out for him to wait, but he shut the door fast but easy, so as not to wake anyone.

I looked around the sparsely furnished bedroom, no pictures on the walls. The wallpaper was peeling, so I made a mental image of all the painting that had to be done.

I went on in my mind as I laid there. Sewing new curtains, maybe drapes? As I concentrated on how beautiful I could make this room appear, my daydreams were cut short when Leslie began to stir in his crib.

I picked him up, and noticed he had an ashen complexion. He seemed listless! Last night he was active and alert. He was so attentive when I sang him to sleep.

I cried, "What's wrong, my little one?" I gently shook him with no real response. A form of hysteria swept over me. "He needs help. He won't wake up."

I ran out of the apartment into the hallway and frantically knocked on my neighbor's door.

"My baby, my baby, something is wrong with him. Please come with me." An older woman, bewildered by my behavior, came directly with me, saying, "What's the matter?"

She looked at my Leslie and said, "Your baby needs a doctor. Quickly, wrap him up and I'll take you to the hospital nearby."

I woke up J.J. and told him to take care of Margaret who was sleeping, saying, "Leslie is ill. I have to leave."

At the hospital my neighbor (a stranger) put her arms around me. "Where is your husband?" she asked. "Do you want me to fetch him for you?"

I looked into her concerned eyes and told her my husband was away. "I don't know how to reach him."

I put my hands into my face and thought to myself I should have never left Hungary. Now I will lose my son.

"Dear God," I prayed, "help my baby, don't take him away from me." I prayed for God to give me strength to bear my cross. "Jesus? I love you! Thy Will be done."

"My children," I said. "I left them alone. How can I leave my Leslie?"

"Don't worry, sweet lady," my neighbor said. "I will go back to the apartment and care for your other children. Right now you need to stay with your baby."

I thanked her and said, "I don't even know your name?"

As she left, she said, "It's Mary. Mary Kelly."

My heart sank... "Mary? My mama's name?" (Mariska in Magyar). "Oh, Mama? You are still watching over me, thank you."

I paced the corridor, waiting nervously for the doctors to tell me how my son Leslie was.

Footsteps in the hallway, slowly approached me. Then hesitation...as if to delay some grave news. Then...the footsteps continued on past me.

A bad report was given to a poor soul in the next stall, whose agony I heard in a loud voice, "No! No...?"

My heart ached for that unknown person.

Just then a nurse came to my side. "Mrs. Tolda?" She bear down on my hand. "The doctor will see you now."

"What about my baby? Will he be all right?" I said.

My heart was pounding, I could feel it beating in my neck; my stomach was twisted in knots when I saw the doctor leaning over my little one examining him.

He looked up when I entered the room. "Mrs. Tolda?"

"Yes! How is my child?" I said, voice trembling.

The doctor spoke in a firm voice. "I'm afraid he is gravely ill. His throbbing arteries are causing a successive contraction on the heart. A sudden inability of the heart to function may cause a heart attack."

"Why?" I screamed. "Why is this happening to him?"

The doctor explained, "Usually this is due to an embolism or an increased blood pressure. I can't be sure in a child so young. It's probably congenital."

"Congenital? What are you saying?"

"It means this existed at birth or from one's birth. I'll see that he's admitted. I'll get back with you later. Will you be here, Mrs. Tolda?" he asked.

"Of course I will," I said with indignation in my voice, "I won't leave his side."

"Good," the doctor said with a half smile on his face.

Mary came back as she promised. "The children are fine, my daughter Bridget is with them," she said. "So don't worry about them. I'm staying here with you."

She put her arms around me and said, "You need to rest, put your head on my shoulder and close your eyes, you

113

look so tired." In the same breath, she said, "Did you find out about your baby?"

"Yes," I said quivering, "he's very sick, he may die."

"Oh no, don't think that way. The doctors here are very good, they will help him."

"I pray you are right, I want to be with him. Why can't I go to him? I waited for hours without seeing him. Oh, my baby, he must be afraid with all those strangers around him."

Finally they let me into his room. My heart almost broke when I saw him.

My baby had machines attached to him, tubes in his mouth to help him breathe, and needles in his little arms. They strapped him in the crib so as not to move.

I held his little hands and prayed for God's help, and fell asleep in the chair next to his crib.

It was morning when the doctor shook my shoulder and said, "We did everything possible for him. He's gone to heaven. I'm awfully sorry, Mrs. Tolda. Is there anything we can do for you?"

"My God, what are you saying? He's dead? He's dead?" I started to shake my baby to wake him up. "Leslie, my baby, don't leave me. Oh! God, I'm going to faint." I grabbed the doctor's lab coat, pinching his skin.

"My baby, what happened to him?"

"Mrs. Tolda, get a hold of yourself," he said. "Nurse! Get me that sedative I prepared for her, quickly."

"No, doctor, I'll be all right. Just let me hold him one more time. Please?" Tears streaming down my face, I said, "He's my baby. I have to hold him and tell him that I love him."

"Yes, Mrs. Tolda, but let us fix him for you. Nurse get that equipment off of him...Now!"

The doctor held me up after the machines were taken away. "Now hold him," he said, "we'll leave you with him.

"Nurse, stand by the door!"

In a stern and commanding voice the doctor said, "She needs time with him...Move! Move!"

Then he said to the nurses, "Let's go!" And... with misty eyes, he shut the door quickly.

I bent down to pick Leslie up. I kissed his chalk colored face and said, "You look just like a little angel sleeping...so sleep, dear heart." My tears fell upon his baby face.

I whispered into his ear, "I'll love you forever."

I don't remember how long I stayed with him. My thoughts of when he was born, his christening, the way he giggled filled my soul. He was a happy baby. "Dear God, please give me the strength to bear this cross."

My Margaret. What can I tell her? "Please give me the words, Dear God. Oh, Joseph, I wish you were here! How can I tell you? Our young son is taken from us."

Mary Kelly had just come into the room, saying she was sorry about Leslie...she kissed me and said, "Mrs., you must go home now. Your other children are waiting for you. I'll help you with the arrangements."

"Mary? How can I leave him? How can I go?"

"You must!" she said. "We'll stop at the desk and make the arrangements, please...let's go, Mrs."

On our way home, I told Mary she was just like an angel sent from heaven. "Mary? How will Joseph react to the loss of another child? I myself cannot bear it. My heart is breaking."

When we reached my home, I placed my hand on the doorknob but could not turn it, I was numb...it seemed like I had no feelings, my anxiety was obvious.

My thoughts went wild. How can I hide my grief from my children? I must try. "Good God, help me. Oh, Joseph where are you?"

When I opened the door, Mary Kelly's daughter greeted me. She was about my age, tall, very pretty with bright red hair. "Mrs. Tolda?" she said, "Hello, I'm Bridget. Everything is fine, Margaret is sleeping; J.J. and Stephen are in the kitchen. So...I'll be leaving now."

She conveyed her condolences and said, "I'm just next door, call me if you need me."

J.J. came running out of the kitchen when he heard me. "Mama? Is it true? Did Leslie die?" His eyes bulged with tension.

"Yes, my darling, it's true! It is true."

We grabbed each other and held tight. Stephen was crying and said, "I know my mother is dead too. Why did God do this to us, you said He loves us, did you lie?"

J.J. spoke up before I could, "God doesn't let this happen because he doesn't love us. We don't know why it happens. It just happens, we have to be strong, right, mama?"

"Right, son." I kissed him with all the love in me.

"Right? J.J., you're right." I thought out loud. "Out of the mouths of babes... 'Train a child the way he will go, and he will not depart from it.' I hope, J.J., your upbringing will comfort you in bad times.

"The world, J.J., will try to change your mind on how you were brought up. Stay strong, defeat evil with good. Always look for the good in everything, because God only made the good. And... yes, He does love us."

"Mama, can I lay down in your bed with you?" J.J. said. "I feel lonely for Leslie tonight."

"Of course you can, you come too, Stephen." J.J. laid on one side and Stephen on the other. They quickly fell asleep. I said, "Thank you, Jesus, for my sweet son, and Stephen too...Jesus? Kiss my baby Leslie for us."

It was a while before I fell asleep. I was going over the arrangement I left with the hospital. Also...what will I tell Joseph?

Morning came soon. All the children were still sleeping, I was grateful for that. How, just how can I live through today. Is this really happening?

Just then I heard the door key turn. Joseph came in. "What's this?" he said in an amused tone. "You're all in bed. Which one was scared of the bogeyman?" He laughed.

Then he looked at my face. "Amelia? What's wrong? You look exhausted." He then looked over at Leslie's crib. "Where is Leslie? What's going on here?"

"Joseph, it's Leslie." I just blurted it out. "Leslie is dead, he's gone." I hunched over holding my head. "My baby is gone!" I was almost hysterical.

Joseph quickly pulled me into the kitchen, whispering so loud in my ear, "What happened?"

I tried to explain to him that, "He was not looking good, he was very pale and couldn't breathe. Our neighbor took us to the hospital, there he died."

Joseph shook me, then pushed me so hard I fell to the floor. "I told you to get a first class cabin, didn't I?" He leaned over me and shouted, "He caught something on the ship. It's all your fault. It's all your fault. My sister told me how you were carrying on with the captain, you left my son all alone, now he's dead."

"How dare you," I shouted back. "Your sister lied to you, she hates me. How can you believe her?"

117

J.J. came running into the kitchen, "Leave her alone." He helped me to my feet. "Mama, are you hurt?"

Margaret woke up with all the noise, she started to cry. I ran into the room to comfort her.

My husband left, slamming the door behind him. After Joseph left, my children crowded around me. That night Margaret came to sleep with me...and then J.J. and Stephen stood by my bed just looking. I beckoned for him to come also.

We all cuddled up together, in silence... Then I started to say my night prayers, they joined in with me. I'm so grateful I have them. What a comfort they are. Oh, if only my little Leslie were here. "Oh, my little Leslie, I miss you so." I could not contain my tears, that poured out an unrelenting flow.

Morning arrived in spite of my fear of it.

Mary Kelly was knocking at my door, softly calling out my name. When I opened the door, she stood there with her arms just loaded down with food. "You had no time to shop, dear girl, so I did it for you. Come let's make breakfast for those hungry children."

I kissed her hand and thanked her a hundred times for being a friend, a true kind friend.

The children bathed and dressed while Mary and I made breakfast. Not a morsel was left on their plates. We laughed and talked as if it were old times again. My heart was lifted in seeing the children act so cheerful.

After breakfast the children left to play in the other room. Mary put her hand on my shoulder and looked me in the eyes. "Amelia? Time to go to the hospital. I called my funeral director to help you. Is that all right with you?"

"Mary, I tried not to think about it. But...yes, thank you for your help."

At the funeral home I was asked if I wanted my little angel waked at the apartment? I quickly answered, "No!"

The director said in a business like manner, "It will cost more."

"No," I said again, "my husband and I want it here. He will be with me to pick out the coffin tonight."

On the way home I confessed to Mary Kelly that I didn't know where my Joseph worked or how I could get in touch with him. "What if he doesn't show up tonight?" I said in an uncontrollable frenzy.

"Hold on to yourself, little lady, hold on! We can do it without his help. I'll have Bridget stay with the children tonight."

I looked at her with adoring eyes and said, "Thank you, mama."

"What did you say, Amelia?"

"Oh, oh, I said thank you."

I waited for such a long time for Joseph to come home. Finally, I told Mary Kelly to come with me to make the arrangements. I couldn't believe Joseph would do this.

Leslie was placed in his little coffin, and I brought a rose to him and said a so-long. Never a good-bye. When I kissed him, my knees were shaking, J.J. held me so as not to fall. He too kissed Leslie.

Stephen bent down, kissed him and said, "It's not your fault, little Leslie, Jesus wanted you now!"

Then it was Margaret's turn. She kissed him and said, "Why is he sleeping so long?"

I tried to explain that God wanted him in heaven, so he could play with the angels.

Margaret wanted to know if she could play with the angels. She said, "Does he want me too?"

"No, not yet, sweet one, not yet!" I held her close...

119

We had the Mass of the Angels at St. Peter's Church. The priest met us at the door of the church and sprinkled the little casket with holy water. A white sheath with a gold cross covered the coffin. We led a procession down the center of the aisle to where my little one faced the altar.

Two candles were placed at the head of the coffin.

I looked for Joseph, but he was nowhere in sight.

The responsory was sung: "Come to his assistance, ye Saints of God; meet him, ye angels of the Lord. Receive his soul, and present it in the sight of the Most High."

I could barely make it to the pew. J.J. and Mary Kelly had to help me.

I sat there watching the candle lit at the head of the tiny casket, it glowed with a flicker of red and gold. I stared at it, so as not to look at the little casket covered with the white scarf.

When it came time for me to receive the Precious Body and Blood of Jesus, I felt the strength sap out of me. The priest looked at me and quickly came over so I would not have to rise from my pew. He gave me my Holy Communion and said, "Hang in there, Amelia, Jesus loves you."

I looked at him, I did not see him...instead...I saw the face of my papa, saying, "Amelia, Say Jesus, I love you and everything will be all right." A surge of strength entered my body.

The thought of my little one with God, and my mama and papa, gave me courage. I held on to my children and walked back to the hearse, my overwhelming sorrow had turned into joy.

Mary Kelly and her husband Ray, and daughter Bridget accompanied us to the cemetery.

At the conclusion of the burial rite at the grave, I felt a hand around my waist. It was Joseph. He turned me around and sobbed uncontrollably in my arms. "Amelia, I am so sorry. Will you every forgive me? I shouldn't have listened to my sister. I love you, forgive me, please?"

He kissed me and the children. And... we all went home.

Since that day at the cemetery, we were brought back together like it used to be. J.J. forgave him, and Joseph promised he would never act that way again.

I explained what had happened to our little son, that it was no ones fault for his short existence in our lives. "Joseph, the doctor said Leslie would have died in Hungary, because of his condition." And...I reminded him and myself of the joy he gave us. And...we drew solace from that thought.

Chapter 11

Becoming an American

We grew closer because of our loss and Joseph showed attention in a loving way.

He had made plans to go on a family vacation. "There's so much beauty to see here and I'm going to show it to you all." The children were thrilled and shouted with joy.

That following week, he borrowed a carriage and we set out to explore Connecticut. Traveling along the roads reminded me of Budapest. It brought back a lot of memories. I loved it.

We stayed at an Inn one night near the Connecticut River. The river divided the state almost in half, like the Danube River did in Hungary.

I wanted to ride the river just like I did years ago in the "old country." Joseph laughed and informed me that the river must be over four hundred miles long. "It begins in northern New Hampshire," he said. "But that's not a bad idea, Amelia. We could start where if flows southward in Connecticut. I think the river's journey empties into the Long Island Sound."

"Someday we'll do it all," he said as he rubbed my hand in his.

On our second night, we stayed at a colonial inn that was one hundred years old. I thought to myself, "Old? Old...is in Europe. This country is just a baby. I love it."

Joseph interrupted my thoughts, saying, "It's getting late, we best start for home."

But before we left for home, Margaret gaped at some white-tailed deer frolicking in the woods. She insisted she wanted to stop and play with them. Papa told her, "Sweetheart, they're shy, they'll run away from you."

Margaret insisted again, "Papa...I love them."

"They love you too, but...from a distance," he said. We all laughed at her amusing facial expressions.

Halfway home the children fell asleep. That gave my husband and I time to talk. I started to ask questions about his job. Like, "Where do you work?" And, "How far is it from home?" Before I could get an answer, he started to tell me about our next trip.

He took a deep breath and said, "I'd like to take you to the largest lake in Western Connecticut. It's called The Candlewood Lake.

"Are you ready for that, Amelia? It's quite a distance?" He chuckled, "We'll probably have to stay a few nights at the inn there. Would you like that, Amelia?"

"Oh yes," I answered as if I didn't notice his reluctance in answering any of my questions. "That would be wonderful," I said.

I started to ask questions about the lake. "Is it like Western Hungary? Like the Balaton Lake?"

Then the tears streamed down my face as I spoke. "Joseph. Remember I told you I was suppose to go there with my family? But I was sick and didn't go?" I started to sob, "They all perished on the way back home from Balaton Lake, remember?"

Joseph tapped my hand, "Amelia, we don't have to go to Candlewood Lake."

"No, no, you don't understand. I need to go. Joseph, I will fulfill my dream if I go. I want to take my family to that beautiful lake. Oh, yes...I want to go!"

Joseph didn't say anymore and neither did I.

On the way home we passed through a valley with its white oak trees, oh...so beautiful. The Mountain Laurel, a flower with its white and pink blossoms had a wonderful smell that saturated the air.

All my senses were aroused. Thoughts of my mama and papa came alive. I could picture mama around her flowers. The feeling of loneliness engulfed my soul. It stayed with me until we arrived home.

When we stopped, Margaret said in a whining voice, "Papa, do we have to go home?" Then with a big yawn, she fell fast asleep again.

We woke the boys up and papa carried Margaret up to the apartment. The moment she was put into her bed, she awoke. A kiss on her cheek and a whisper...shush, and she fell fast asleep again.

Mary Kelly knocked on the door, she handed me a letter that came to her by mistake. It was from my Aunt Irene, my hand shook when I opened it. My eyes fell on the sentence, "Amelia, when should I send you the rest of your estate money?"

My skeptical instinct told me to peruse the letter and guard its contents. I quickly thought, Joseph is not being forthright with me. I feel he is holding a secret, I must wait.

I tucked the letter into my pocket and said, "I'll read it later."

Joseph looked at me and asked if everything was all right. Then he said in a muffled voice, "Did she mention when she would be sending your estate money?"

"What did you say, Joseph?" I pretended not to have heard him.

"Nothing," he said. "I was talking to myself. I want to get something to eat." He walked into the kitchen.

That night in each other's arms, we talked about how great the trip was and how the children loved seeing the sights. We agreed we should do this again real soon.

Nothing was said about my letter, or the questions I had asked him about his job.

After our loving, we went to sleep. In the middle of the night, I saw Joseph searching my pocket for the letter. I...had it under my pillow.

The morning was bright with sunshine and we all got an early start on a new day. We went to church, had a great dinner, enjoyed our moments together, wishing it would never end. Nevertheless, our wonderful day was almost over.

Hurrying, Joseph got ready to leave for work again. I helped him pack his clothes in silence.

On leaving, Joseph kissed us, saying, "I'll be home next week, Amelia? I'll send my brother by to check up on you and the children. Will that be all right?"

I nodded yes, and waved good-bye.

Afterwards I read the letter from my Aunt Irene. She spoke of how the village had changed, and the turmoil they were going through. "There's so many reform groups springing up it scares me," she wrote.

"Meanwhile," she said, "we are getting ready to sell what we can and leave here. There's no man around here to protect us, and we're afraid for our lives."

I wrote back telling her, "Your letter gives me some concern. Please do not worry about my estate money. If you need to use it, do so...don't do without."

I went on... "Margaret is so beautiful, J.J. and Leslie are growing so tall. Everyone is fine." I never mentioned the death of our little son, Leslie, whom she loved so much. Why add to her grief? What purpose would it serve?

To sum my letter up, I lead her to believe my new life was blissful. No room for anguish or sorrow...

Signing off on a humorous note, telling her all the funny things the children were doing, I closed...

"All our love, Amelia."

Days seemed to gallop by, since Ellis Island. The loss of my son weighed heavy in my heart, now...thoughts of losing my husband were there too. I tried to dismiss my feelings and pull myself together and plan for Margaret's third birthday, August 21st. The celebration included Julia...I held out the "proverbial olive branch" reluctantly. Now it was up to her.

The day had arrived. Margaret was so excited on being three, she was now grownup (she said).

Julia didn't come...My husband said she was sick. To me she was a very...sick person.

We had a wonderful party, in spite of her absence.

Mary Kelly and the rest of our neighbors praised my baking. They loved the birthday cake and asked if I would bake for them sometime (if I wanted to make extra money).

In the morning, I awoke feeling very tired. The very thought of making breakfast made me feel nauseous. But...I got up and scurried into the kitchen.

I had the bread in the oven stove making toast, and was busy setting the table. When all of a sudden my husband ran out into the kitchen, "Is there a fire?" he yelled. Then he took the burning bread out of the oven.

Joseph looked so angry and remarked, "Can't you do anything right?"

I ran over to the sink and lost the coffee I had just consumed moments before.

Still looking angry, he said, "What's wrong with you, Amelia? Are you sick?"

I probably looked pale for him to say, "Sit down, I'll fix breakfast."

The children came out to eat and watching them made me feel worse. I left to retire to my bed.

My head revolved like a spinning wheel. I threw myself on the bed crying, not so much because I felt ill, but because of the way Joseph spoke to me. I fell asleep, only to awake with Margaret jumping on my bed.

"Where's papa?" I asked.

"He left for work," she said, as she played with my hair.

His meanness, played over and over in my mind. As weeks went by I still felt sick, especially in the morning. A visit to a doctor confirmed my notion that I had conceived. My baby, he said, would be due in late March or early April.

When I told Joseph, he seemed happy. I know I was.

It was an answer to my prayer. My ache for my Leslie seemed a little lighter.

As time slipped by, Joseph's working hours became longer. The promise he made to me earlier seemed empty by his actions. His reason? "There'll be another mouth to feed."

No matter what his reason, I was determined to be happy and stay healthy, especially now... for the new life I carried. My thoughts soared, thinking about a sweet coddling baby in my arms once more.

In the meantime, I kept busy with reading everything I could get my hands on about my new wonderful country.

I took the children to the library. Margaret kept busy with the juvenile books the Librarian gave her to look at. J.J. and Stephen browsed happily, in spite of the fact they knew no English. Seeing how anxious they were to learn encouraged me to teach them to speak and read the language of their new country. Oh, yes they will be good Americans, and the best citizens. I'll see to that.

Summer was over, now it was time for school. I enrolled them in a Hungarian school first, in order for them to learn English.

I studied with them and made up word games so it would be a pleasant experience for them to learn and remember. I was amazed that in no time they excelled in the language. And soon they were attending public school. Their grades were B and B+, I was very satisfied.

Mary Kelly watched the children while I attended night school to become an American citizen.

Theodore Roosevelt was President and a Republican. It seemed everyone was a Republican. Soon I would vote too.

Then came the day I raised my right hand to defend this country and was made a citizen. I was very proud of myself. My heart almost burst with joy the day we were each given a little flag I will cherish forever.

When I brought it home, Margaret wanted to play with it. She soon found out she could just look at it. It was put in a place of honor and revered.

When Joseph found out I was a citizen, he became outraged to think a woman would do this on her own without asking her husband.

I quietly snapped back at him, "This is America, not the old country. They say in America that women do have rights, that I'm a person, a human being. I'm not owned by anyone...God owns me."

I shocked myself speaking out like this. This new me felt funny. I thought, "Am I sinful?" Sister Mary's voice resounded from the past, "No!" I then became assertive.

I told the children from now on we will speak English, not Hungarian. Joseph did not go along with that, even when I told him he spoke in broken English.

"I'll help you," was the wrong thing to tell this stubborn man, who said he knew everything.

He was white with anger when he said, "How dare you speak to me this way. I'm the head of this house, you do what I say!" He was so angry I didn't dare answer him.

For days he did not speak to me. He spoke through J.J. in Hungarian, when he wanted to ask me something. Then in English I answered, and J.J. told papa in Hungarian.

At times I laughed, because it was funny, but...then it lasted too long. Finally I said in Hungarian to Joseph, "You're acting like a child, this is not good for the children to see."

He said a nasty word to me and left the house, slamming the door. The children looked bewildered at papa's actions.

J.J. asked, "Why is papa always so angry? Mama, doesn't he love us anymore?"

"J.J.," I said, "we must help papa, he has a lot on his mind. He loves us. We just have to keep loving him."

I kissed his forehead, saying, "We must pray for understanding and wisdom. Sometimes, J.J., people go on for years not understanding each other. Remember, J.J., that word: UNDERSTANDING? It brings knowledge of the person we want to be close to.

"A revelation of this human being is then exposed to you. And…only then, you can sympathize with their actions, and willfully compromise.

"Remember! It's because of the lack of understanding why people don't get along.

"So, let's try and understand why papa is acting this way. All right, J.J.? Please?"

"Mama," J.J. said with a puzzled look on his face, "I'll try to understand…what you just said." Then he laughed, saying, "Will I talk like you when I grow up?"

It dawned on me…what I was saying was for myself to hear. In any event…I'll call time, my friend, and wait for a chance to mend our family.

Meantime my children became closer to me, relying on me for everything. This was not my wish. I had to do something to get Joseph involved with his children's lives once again.

I decided to speak to Julia, perhaps she knew the solution to my problem. Just maybe Joseph told her what's troubling him? I wondered where she was staying now.

Curiosity sprang up when I questioned Joseph. He would not tell me of her whereabouts. "Was this a deep dark secret?" I joked with him. "Is it because she's a spy?" I began to laugh so hard, I had a pain in my side. "I happened to know she works for you." I laughed again and he took my arm and twisted it.

"Now? Keep laughing," he said. "Keep laughing and I'll twist it off!"

Then he saw what he was doing and backed off, saying, "Amelia, I'm sorry. Did I hurt you? Forgive me?

"Amelia, I'm going away for a few days. I need to be alone. I can't act this way with you. You're too good."

I agreed with Joseph that he should get away and think about his behavior. And...I needed to think also.

"Joseph," I said, "don't you ever touch me in that way again, ever!" I held the door open for him to leave.

The next day I decided to turn my thoughts elsewhere. During my months with child, I tried to keep busy with a special project. Mainly helping Stephen locate his mother. He worried about her and had so many questions...and I didn't have the answers.

My first apprehension was Elizabeth died. I did not hear from her, or...of her. Did she make it back to Hungary safely? Where is she now?

They were tormenting questions that needed answers.

I turned to the library, perhaps they had the key on how to find out who could help me?

The librarian told me to write to my congressman, senators, and anyone who will listen. So...

Obtaining their names, I set out to tell the story of Elizabeth, and how her son Stephen is grieving in not knowing the fate of his beloved mother.

Many of the letters went unanswered. The ones that replied led me on a trail that came to a dead end.

Still...I continued my investigation relentlessly.

That is, until my baby was born. Six pounds, four ounces, nineteen inches long. She had short black hair (almost bald). And she was adorable.

Amelia Everything Will Be All Right

We named her after me, Amelia Theresa. She had a small mouth and dark brown eyes, and long lashes. I love her, to me she was beautiful. God's gift.

Joseph made a party for the birth of our new child, and we invited...Julia!

I was having a swell time until Julia said, "The baby didn't look like anyone in our family. Does she, Joseph? Are you sure it's yours?"

I was so offended by all of her snide remarks, my thoughts were sinful. And...I told her so.

But Joseph didn't get angry at her. He said with a smile, "She's beautiful. She looks just like her mother." That made me so happy, especially after he added that with a kiss.

When I had a chance, I asked Julia why she hated me so. She told me I broke up her family, and I made a fool out of Joseph by acting like a hussy when men were around, like on the ship with the Captain. It was then she told me Joseph knows everything, "He's sorry he married you. He told me so."

That night I told Joseph what Julia said. He said she was crazy and not to listen to her. "I love you and the children." That night he showed me how much he really loved me.

I was contented with that answer, and for a time we were happy. Julia's name never came up.

Soon after Amelia was born, Margaret, then four, was pushed off a fence and broke her neck. Hospitalized and in a great deal of pain, she kept asking for me. But...they would not let me see her. They said she was not allowed to move her neck for fear it would not mend properly.

I stayed at the hospital night after night and slept in the waiting room.

Then one morning, a nurse came out to speak to me about Margaret crying out in Hungarian, the same thing over and over again. Phonetically the nurse repeated what Margaret was saying, "Kell Vez...Adish Unyum."

I put my hands to my face and cried, "Oh my sweet child is saying, "I want water, sweet mother."

Eventually they let me see her and give her some water. "Mama, I missed you, don't leave me," she said.

The big tears that came from her could have filled the glass I was holding. I kissed her, saying, "I won't, sweetheart. Don't be afraid, Jesus loves you. Remember?"

They all loved Margaret in the hospital. She was there for such a long spell recuperating from the fractured neck...but, she mended well, and as children do...she rallied.

Still stuttering and very shy, but always smiling. I think that's why they loved her so much.

While Margaret regained her strength, I took up the task of finding out about Stephen's mother.

Chapter 12

Off to Washington, D.C.

Finding out about Stephen's mother became a priority. I had gotten in touch with a representative from Ellis Island, inquiring about the ship that left the Island on July 5, 1906, with Elizabeth Hornack on board.

That summer of 1908 I was put in touch with a Mr. Warren Grey, an officer at Ellis Island. My appointment was in the first week of August, the children were out of school...a perfect time to go.

Mary Kelly came with me to help with the children and packed a basket of food, saying, "We can make a picnic out of this ordeal. Right, Mrs?"

The train ride to New York City was fun, the children loved it. But when it came to the ferry ride over to Ellis, I felt a strange sensation. I knew J.J. and Stephen felt it too. Margaret kept asking when the boat ride would be over, she cried until we landed.

Mary Kelly stayed with the children on the first floor and took them to the cafeteria while I went ahead.

I almost felt disoriented when I climbed the stairs to the second floor. Memories came flooding into my mind of the time spent there. I could hear the chatter and rumpus, it was oh, so real. I sat on a familiar bench and waited to be called.

A warm hand touched my shoulder. My heart shuddered with joy to see those dark eyes again still filled with compassion. It was the Captain of our ship.

I explained why I was there and asked for his help. He remembered Stephen and put his arms around me. "I'll help, I knew the difficult time he had, it was tough leaving his mother.

"Wait here!" he said. "I can pull some strings to get your questions answered."

He came back in less than an hour. "It will take a day or two to get your answers, but we'll get them. Meanwhile, let me have your address, Amelia, I'll get word to you there." And...with an expression of respect, he kissed my face saying. "You're a beautiful person, I admire you. God bless you. I'll walk down the stairs with you. I'd like to see the children." On seeing Stephen, he said to him, "Take care, God has His Plan, be strong, we'll find your answers, son."

The very next day I heard Mary Kelly speaking to someone in the hallway with a regretful tone in her voice. Then a heavy knock came at the door, my heart pounded rapidly as I opened it.

There stood the Captain. Both Mary Kelly and he had a somber look on their faces.

I knew when I saw the Captain's face I would be hearing devastating news. Mary Kelly held my hand while I was told the grim details of Elizabeth's death.

The captain hung his head low as he said, "She was buried at sea on the second day out. I understand she was given the Sacrament of Last Rites before she left this hard world." Tears gathered in his brown eyes, then he offered to tell Stephen about his mother.

"Perhaps that would be best if I told him. You know a man's touch. I'll be gentle with him, I lost my mother when I was a boy. I know how it is."

Stephen was called in from playing, and the Captain took him into the bedroom and shut the door. It seemed like a long time before they appeared with arms around each other.

Dusk had fallen and we were all around the dining room table, consoling and remembering.

Stephen came over to me and gave me a big hug, saying, "My mama knew this would happen, and she gave me you."

He leaned over to kiss me, and a large tear fell in my mouth, salty, yet sweet, "I love you, mama," he said.

"Stephen, I love you too, as if you were my very own son, and now you are." We kissed, and we all gathered around each other hugging and crying.

The captain broke away and said, "I do have some good news to tell you all." He reached into his side pocket and pulled out a photo of his wife and son (just born).

"Amelia, you played a large part in my being happy today. After seeing how badly the steerage passengers were treated for so many years, I became bitter and disgusted with everyone. The love you've shown to a stranger, and your willingness to take this child under your care, showed me the goodness in people once again.

"I opened my heart to love again and found my wife. I have you to thank for that.

"Amelia, do you remember I spoke to you about the Foreign Service Officer, Fiorello LaGuardia? I told him all about you. He wants to know if you would go to Washington, D.C. and tell the Congressional Committee all about the steerage passengers. Tell them exactly what you saw. Would you?"

"Me? I'm just an immigrant," I said.

"Amelia!" he said. "What do you mean, just...! Do you know what that word really means? It means fair-minded, impartial, trustworthy, incorrupt, all of these are you. If there were ever a principled person in the world it would be you. Will you be willing to go next month? If so, I'll set up a time schedule and get in touch with you."

"Captain, I made a promise to myself that I would do everything I could, if I had the chance. Yes, I'll go!"

After we finished our talks on an approach to the committee, we decided on a campaign that would make the public aware of the devastating conditions the steerage passengers had to endure.

"This is going to be big...Amelia, you could make a great difference in the outcome."

I was elated when the Captain walked me to the door. "Finally," I said, "an amendment put on the books, preventing such inhumanity from happening again." My grin was enormous.

The Captain held my hand tight, saying, "Amelia, I wish that were so, but this will only slow it down a bit. Brutality will go on until we learn to love one another."

With that, he bent down and kissed me. "See you in D.C.," he said.

He turned to leave and ran smack into Julia and my brother-in-law. Both had their mouths opened wide.

"Julia?" I said, "do you remember the Captain?"

With a sickened look at both of us, she said, "Yes." And shoved a belated birthday gift for Margaret in my hands. "I know who he is...come on James, let's go!" They both stormed away.

"Who are those people?" the captain asked.

"Those people are the kind of people you spoke of before. They have not learned to love. I imagine they will run to my husband and try to make trouble for me."

I told the Captain not to worry about Julia, because nothing will stop me now. "This is my quest. A journey into life I cannot turn back from, nor will I."

The day had arrived. I received all the information I needed from the Captain. So...I was off to Washington.

Mary Kelly asked if I was nervous about the trip, and if I was scared, speaking in front of all those important people. I answered, "Will I be scared? Yes! All of that and more. Guaranteed...my knees will be shaking.

"Mary, I am determined to do the right thing, I have to speak out for all of the special people in steerage I knew. So...Washington, D.C., here I come."

Joseph was angry I was going. He tried to discourage me, saying I was going to make a fool out of myself and the family. "They'll call you a stupid immigrant, you'll see."

I told him how important this was for me to do this. "And...if they choose to call me names? They will look bad, not me." I left without his blessings.

The Captain , Mr. LaGuardia, two men and a woman met me at the station.

My knees were...shaking (just like I said) as we climbed the enormous marble stairs to a magisterial looking building. Inside were statues of various people in high office, and lots of flags.

A long corridor led to a large door. We sat at a wide table with nametags on it.

As I sat at this wide table, I asked the Good Lord for the correct words to come out of my mouth, for my accent to be understood, for my memory to be sharpened.

While all of this was going on in my mind…nine men took their seats on an elevated bench. Looking at me, they searched my face, in their role as the scrutinizing officials.

I raised my right hand and made an oath to the Almighty to tell the truth as I knew it.

The chairman of the committee questioned me first. "Recollect if you will, the first time you were on the orlap deck."

"The orlap deck? Sir, I don't know what that is?"

He answered, "It's below the – deck, proximity to the steering apparatus (sigh!), in other words, it's located in the very bottom of the vessel."

"Oh…! Yes sir, do you mean where the steerage passengers were?"

He seemed annoyed with me and said, "Uh, hum, yes, that's what I mean."

At first I felt intimated by his lack of intolerance towards me. And then I remembered I wanted to do something for these courageous immigrants that suffered so much misery. So I gathered up some courage…Now was the time to help them. Gallantly…I started to speak out loud and clearly.

"It was very dirty down there and no air, I mean no fresh air to breath. Their hatches were fastened down most of the time. And…if they didn't bring their own food, well, woe to them. Some of the people were covered with lice they didn't even bother to remove them. It seemed hopeless, I guess, because they would only jump back on them again, especially the ones that were too sick to wash up.

"The foul water was so salty and hard, it would make them itch more, and they had to drink that water too."

Then I examined the faces of the nine men sitting there. They were not moved at what I had just said.

Looking at the Chairman again I asked, "Isn't there a limit on the number of passengers a ship could carry? Didn't the United States government set these limits?"

The Chairman answered with a half smile, "We will ask the questions, Mrs. Tolda...continue on with what you saw!"

I did not let them see the frustration that was building up in me. I calmly answered, "I saw passengers crammed tightly into the very bottom of the ship. A mother and her young child slept near the rudder. The noise was deafening, yet she didn't complain...Who would listen? I found out later she kept holding the child close to her after the child had died. They didn't even bother to take the child from her until the stench became unbearable. Help for them came too late...

"It was very depressing to see such hopelessness. There was sickness and suffering amidst them. The want of food, the thirst, dampness, heat and anxiety was beyond belief.

"Some prayed when a storm hit that it would end all their anguish."

I went on for almost two hours with no intermission or interruption.

After the committee hearing, I left the Great Hall with a feeling of helplessness myself. Would they do something? Did they listen to me and understand? Did they care?

The Captain said yes to all of my questions. He patted me on the back and said, "You were very...persuasive."

Mr. LaGuardia sat close to me and said, "It takes time, Amelia. You were the last one to speak and they let you speak the longest, I might add…you're creditable. I saw many people wipe away tears. You touched them, and they listened to you!"

Just then a flood of reporters gathered around me. "Spell your last name, Amelia!" one shouted out – after that I was immersed with questions. Flashes of light from their cameras blinded me. The Captain pushed his way through the gang of reporters with me in front of him. "Make way," he yelled, "give her some breathing room."

Later the Captain with his lovely family, and Mr. LaGuardia took me to dine in a posh Washington restaurant.

"They haven't heard the last of us," Mr. LaGuardia said. "Amelia? You were just wonderful," he continued. "You're smart! Smart, not to make men feel uncomfortable." He laughed, "are you sure you're not a politician? Your womanly ways are refreshing. You reminded me of the women that rode out west with their men. Bold and daring, unafraid to take a step into the wildness, and willing to take the risk with them. I commend you."

Then the Captain spoke, raising his glass, he said, "Hear, hear. Speak, Amelia, what do you have to say?"

I stood up and said, "Thank you for all of your compliments. I was sitting here listening to all these wonderful things you're saying about me. As you see, my face is reddening with each word of praise from all of you.

"I should not be praised for something most women, most mothers, would do. I did nothing. I only spoke the truth. I happen to be a woman who loves the truth.

"I wish to thank you all for caring for the less fortunate, the ones whose voices could not be heard over the money changers.

"This is a great country, mainly because of the diversity of its people. And therefore, a person like me...an immigrant can have a chance to be heard. I thank you one and all. And...God Bless America."

There was a great applause and I stood there humbled and, of course, blushing. I felt like I was glued to the floor. I couldn't move. The Captain realizing what had happened to me, came up and escorted me to my chair. I was so grateful.

Afterwards we had a wonderful reception. I shook so many hands, I felt like a celebrity or someone running for office.

Hours later we made our way to the train station.

Again I thanked them all, still not believing this was happening to me.

When the train started, I sank down into the seat near the window, waved and watched them disappear from sight.

I shut my eyes and thought, Joseph would be proud of me...proud I was his wife.

See, Joseph? I didn't make a fool out of myself or our family. I spoke up because I'm an American...who belongs to the Human Family.

Chapter 13

Margaret's Visions

Summer passed quickly and it was now October. The headlines of the local paper read:

October 6, 1908 - THE FIRST BALKAN CRISIS – Austria annexes Herzegovina and Bosnia.

As I read on, I was fearful for my Aunt Irene and Ellen. Disturbing news kept coming in about the troubles in Europe.

I immediately wrote to them and asked them to come to America where they would be safe. I never received an answer to my letter.

At the end of the month I learned that I was in the family way. I was happy that the Lord had blessed us again, but, the foreboding war in Europe upset me so that my blood pressure became very high.

The doctor told Joseph I needed to relax and unburden myself. "Take her for a ride through the hills away from the city and worry," he told him.

So Joseph packed us up, and, in a borrowed carriage, we were on our way.

Joseph knew how much I loved George Washington, the first president of our country (I even took his birth date, February 22nd, mine is February 23rd). So...

We went to Washington in Litchfield County. It was the first town in the United States to be named for George Washington. And, I wanted to see it.

Washington lies sheltered amid the hills of Litchfield, and on the tour we were told it was incorporated in 1779.

At the time I didn't know what that meant so I said, "Oh, how wonderful they had it blessed. This must be holy ground." Laughter from people in the background made me realize that's not what it meant, so I laughed too.

I was taught that if you laugh at yourself, you wouldn't appear so stupid. Looking back on my life, I guess I accomplished that, because I laugh a lot.

But you know what? I wasn't far from wrong, for it was holy ground. Many brave men were buried there.

Anyway I felt connected to the scenery. Litchfield reminded me of Miskolc, Hungary, where I was born. The delightful rolling hills, which are part of the Taconic Mountains, took me back to when I was a young girl.

This was a great time to get close to God and nature. Life is too short not to have your children enjoy God's gifts of a beautiful world. We loved our trip so much, we started to make plans to travel like this again. Joseph agreed this was what we all needed.

That night we stayed at a charming old inn, the visit there did relax me. Joseph relaxed too.

The next day we started out for home, and as soon as we neared home, Joseph's attitude changed.

It was like he was two different people.

"This trip has cost me a lot of money. I'll have to go back to work tonight," he said. So he took his suitcase and vanished with not even a good-bye...to me, or the children.

It was sad this had happened, for it spoiled the happy feelings we all had before. So...I told the children we are now going to have a party. Then the children perked up again. I invited Mary Kelly and her family over and we all had a wonderful time. We played our music and sang happy songs. The children went to bed happy and thanking Jesus for such a great vacation.

We spent many nights alone after our trip. J.J. took over the job his papa should have done.

That Christmas Eve we were alone with no Christmas tree for my children...with no sign of Joseph showing up. And...it was snowing hard, the weather was getting worse. That's when I decided to get the tree myself.

"The children will have a Christmas tree when they wake up on Jesus' birthday," I said. "Come snow or high water."

My feet were very swollen, so I asked my son to help me put my boots on.

"Mama!" he said. "There's no need for boots. Stephen and I will pick a tree up for us. I'm not letting you go out in this weather, I'm sorry...Let's go, Stephen."

Before I could say no, they were out the door.

They brought back a tree so large that Mr. Kelly had to chop the top off to get it through the door. We joked a lot about it while we trimmed the tree.

It was a wonderful Christmas, regardless of their papa not showing up. We had laugher, gifts, and each other.

I rang in the New Year, 1909 without Joseph. He came home three days after the holidays. He told the children he was sorry, but it was not his fault, it was because of the weather. Without bitterness in their hearts and no gifts in papa's hands, the children were happy to see him, in spite of his excuses.

Weeks went by with nothing happening, except I was getting bigger and lonelier and…William Howard Taft became President, his inauguration was March 4, 1909.

I daydreamed that I was there telling him how I voted for the first time. And I was so happy he chose me to be the first woman Vice President for his running mate. The President raised my hand with his to the crowds in a victory gesture. The bands were playing, flags were flying.

Just think. Me! Amelia…Vice President of these United States.

Oh, how foolish daydreams can be…but oh, what fun.

Months later I received a letter from the Captain. He wrote, "I have some good news for you. A commission investigator confirmed what you said concerning the sleeping space for the steerage passengers."

The Captain continued writing about what the investigators found. He wrote, "The stench from the nearby toilets were being checked, thanks to you, Amelia. I know it was almost impossible to keep one's self clean. I still don't know how you did it, Amelia. Your family always looked nice. I felt hurt for everyone that couldn't do what you did."

He thanked me again, saying, "This may take years, Amelia, maybe only little things will be done. But, at least we tried to do the right thing, and that's all God asks of all of us." He closed by saying, "Will keep you informed. God bless you and yours," Robert.

I was busy the following months, busy knitting and crocheting baby things, getting ready for the blessed event.

The wonderful hour had arrived, our child was born on a hot sticky, summer's day, July 17, 1909.

He was so big, with lots of hair and long legs. I loved him before he was born, can you imagine how much I loved him now?

We named him Alexander, after Joseph's great uncle. His uncle was known for his great kindness to the poor. Some said he was a saint. He had enormous piety and humility. The traits I had wished for our son.

We now had five wonderful children. Stephen was 14, J.J. was ten, Margaret six, Amelia two, and now Alek.

When Alek was just a month old, Joseph planned a vacation before the children went back to school. "We are all going to the largest lake in Connecticut," he said. "Plenty of White Oak trees and the flowers you love, Amelia, the Mountain Laurel."

We packed quickly and left in a hurry (just in case Joseph would change his mind).

When we arrived at Candlewood Lake, I was dazzled by the splendor of it all. This certainly was as lovely as Joseph said.

Papa went sailing with J.J. and Stephen, the rest of us stayed near the river's edge. Amelia and I dangled our feet in the water, while Margaret held Alek and just watched.

We listened to the robins singing. And when we got too near them, they started their warbling song as a signal warning that we were intruders. We backed away and just listened.

Margaret explained to Alek what the robins were doing, and what song they were singing.

After lunch we stayed at an inn in Danbury. We had a wonderful dinner and at night Joseph was so romantic.

I gave up trying to figure him out, I just savored every moment we had together. Thank you, Jesus, for having him come back to me, was my prayer. I loved him so much that I guess I would always forgive him. Even though he blamed others for his mistakes.

In the morning we started out for home. We drove by the Connecticut River and J.J. and Stephen yelled out to papa that they spotted some beavers.

We stopped to watch them as they used the large incisor teeth to cut wood for their dwellings. J.J. said they lived in family groups, "And they work together, Papa." Joseph gave me a queer look, and we started out again.

Next we stopped and watched river otters up the bank. Margaret laughed at their short legs and flat tails. Their dark brown fur coat was shining, "They're beautiful," Margaret said. "Papa, I want one."

Then Papa said, "I could make a nice fur hat out of them." Margaret started to cry. "I'm only fooling, Margaret," papa said, and picked her up and kissed her.

We all started to laugh, even Margaret did. We had such a good time that I wanted to freeze that moment and lock it away in my memories. I didn't want these days to end.

When we arrived home, the children went to bed early. The night was ours. Joseph took me out on the veranda and looked up at the stars and counted each one. "See how many stars there are, Amelia, that is how much I love you."

Joseph distracted me by talking about what had happened on our vacation. He was laughing and kissing me constantly.

Little did I know he had Mary Kelly set a bottle of wine out and a lovely bunch of flowers to grace the table. Some leftovers were put out on my best dishes, with a lit candle to make the scene romantic.

When he walked me inside, he said, "This is our time, Amelia," he kissed my lips and held me tight.

"This was a wonderful vacation just like old times back in Hungary," he said. "Sometimes, Amelia, I wish we were still there." His eyes filled with care, saying, "I want to give you so much, but I don't know how."

"Joseph?" I said, "tell me what's wrong, why do you feel that way?"

"I don't know, Amelia. I guess I listen to Julia too much. She really doesn't like you. She says you hold me back because we have this large family and one of them isn't mine."

"True, Stephen is not yours. But you love him, don't you? He's a good boy, we're all he has. He's like our own son. Tell your sister to learn to love God more, then she'll learn to love others and stop making trouble for us."

"Amelia," Joseph said in bated breath, "let this be our night." He picked me up and carried me into the bedroom and shut the door.

Life was beautiful again, everything was going right for a change. And...my husband loves me.

Joseph came home every night, and the children played with him. For the first time in a very long time I felt we were a family again.

Joseph came home one night, excited about a new apartment he found for us. "It's a large apartment with three bedrooms, lots of room for us all," he said.

So we moved to Ward Street in Hartford.

We were living there for a few months and everything was going fine. The children adjusted to their new environment.

Until one day Margaret came running into the house, she was frantic. It was just turning dark and she was coming

149

in from playing when she saw a man and woman going down into the cellar. "She had a wedding gown on, and he was wearing a black suit (tuxedo)...they were holding each other and kissing. Mama, they didn't have a face."

The cold chills went through me as Margaret spoke. I could see she was afraid...This time she scared me, because the cellar was never used by anyone, and the door to it...was rusted closed.

"Mama, mama," she continued, "they didn't open the door, they went through it, and I didn't see them anymore. What happened to them?"

I told her she had a great imagination, and that's all it was...In my heart I was frightened, that night she slept in my bed.

There was another incident the following year. It was January and very cold. Margaret stayed home from school with a cold. I was in the kitchen and Margaret was sitting in a window seat, facing Ward Street.

We had a great big tree in front of the apartment. When Margaret was sitting in the window seat, she said she was thinking about what she was missing in school. Then her eyes focused on the giant tree, she rubbed her eyes and tried to adjust them to see clearly because she couldn't believe what she had just seen.

"At the root of the giant tree, the ground opened up and a black box appeared. Things were flying out of it." She said she couldn't tell what it was.

"Then a lot of people came around, picked up what appeared to be coins and bills...the people looked like they were overwhelmed, trying to gather what they could.

"They were almost in hysteria..." Before she could realize what had happened, they disappeared.

She came running to me and yelling to "come see," of course, when I looked out the window, I saw nothing.

Oh, my poor little girl, I wrapped her in my arms and rocked back and forth. "Dear Jesus, please help her."

That night after dinner, I left to talk to Mrs. Cowel. She had lived here in the apartment building for many years. And, being up in age...she had much wisdom. Perhaps she could shed some light on what was happening to my little girl.

When I told her what Margaret had seen, she was stunned. "Amelia? Not your daughter too. I also had that same experience. You see, years ago there was a murder here in this apartment building!

"The murdered couple had just gotten married, and they had a black suitcase. And it had all their savings, jewelry, and tickets to the Islands for their honeymoon in it. That black case was never recovered...

"The newspapers carried the story, and hoards of people came around. They even dug up the grounds. They were yelling...all pandemonium broke out...It was bedlam.

"I was the only one that stayed in the neighborhood after that, everyone said this house was haunted and the couple will never rest until the assailants were apprehended."

I went home thinking to myself, perhaps Mrs. Cowel had told Margaret this story...and Margaret unconsciously had her imagination run away with her?

Only a couple of days went by and Margaret had another experience. This time it was in her bedroom. In the upper corner of the ceiling was a bright light; a statue of the Infant Jesus appeared there. She came running out of the room to me, shaking and crying.

Maybe this is a sign, I thought...We must move.

Joseph was angry that I wanted to move. He said, "Julia said what she needs is a good spanking, all this is nonsense."

"Julia? What does she know about children? The health of our girl comes first. We...are moving."

Joseph left the house and didn't come home for days.

And so we moved that following month. I found a rent on Sanford Street in Hartford. It was a three family brick house; the Gillands owned it. We had the second floor. We had plenty of space, the rooms were very large, much larger than on Ward Street.

The Kelly family helped us move. I thank God for them every day.

Joseph showed up and liked the apartment, so everything was normal again.

Weeks later I received a letter from Captain Robert. He told me about the Dillingham Commission and all the improvements that had been made.

"The new-type steerage is a modified second class cabin, simpler and plainer accommodations. Also, separate staterooms are being provided, two to eight berths in each, just like you had.

"And...Amelia? The sanitary conditions are better than the old-type, but...it still lacks good ventilation. But at least the crowding is eliminated.

"By the way, Amelia, in October, Mr. LaGuardia gave up his interpreter job. You know, for two years he did a lot for the steerage passengers.

"He also worked on the Board of Inquiry and Medical Wards. Too bad he wasn't there when Elizabeth Hornack (Stephen's mother) was there. Oh well, I'm sure she's in Heaven, she was a good woman.

"Fiorello never ceased to speak out to the Washington Authorities with suggestions. You know, Amelia, his ideas for improvement of the clearance system were great, and he intervened for heartbreaking cases, like Elizabeth.

"He was there, showing them kindness and consideration when needed.

"Sometimes, I think he's a saint, like you.

"Now he's studying real hard to be a lawyer. Being a part-time law student, he's helping the new immigrants in the Manhattan Night Court.

"He sure is a hard worker, thank God.

"Well, take care, Amelia, keep praying for those poor souls. And...me."

Your friend, Robert.

Whom you helped change (for the better).

Our family sends their love to your family.

Taken in 1912 - (left to right).
J.J. age 13, Alek 3, Amelia 5, &
Margaret 9.
Stephen was 17, and did not join
in the family picture.
The following year Joseph left
us again...

Chapter 14

Joseph Leaves Us

It was a balmy evening with the slow descent of the sun below the horizon. Margaret was out playing with her pet when suddenly she heard a loud noise in the sky that made her look up. "It was like thunder," she said. "I saw a chariot, it had two wheels – with four or six horses. A man was standing with reins in his hands. He drove very fast across the sky, then disappeared." In a child-like manner, she described a Roman soldier, wearing a helmet and an armor breastplate.

It was days before Margaret told me of this incident. Questioning her further, I decided to take her to see a priest. I told the good Father she was only ten years old this past week (her birthday was August 21st). I was frightened by her vision and wanted him to bless her.

He asked Margaret many questions, and he listened intently to her answers. Then with an affectionate embrace, he kissed her head.

The priest looked into my eyes and said, "Amelia, as the story goes, there was a war in heaven between good and evil. Perhaps the two-wheeled vehicle was used?"

The priest continued, "You know the same kind of chariot Margaret said she saw? Anyway, St. Michael the Archangel did battle with Lucifer, the prince of darkness and he, Satan, was banished from the third heaven to the heavens, one and two below.

"If one opens up the Bible to: The Apocalypse, Chapter 20, verse 3, they would read: 'And he cast him into the bottomless pit and shut him up and set a seal upon him, that he should no more seduce the nations till the thousand years be finished. And after that, he must be loosed a little time.'

"Perhaps this was a sign from God to the world – a warning that Satan was loosed and was about to rain havoc on the world below.

"Perhaps there will be a War – perhaps it could be avoided. Perhaps its message is that man should seek peace, for it is the absence of evil...

"Margaret may have the ability to see God's revelations, which symbolizes The Divine Truth.

"Your girl seems blessed with Wisdom, she was allowed to see this sign – you are also – blessed to have such a child like her. I don't know what God has in store for your youngster.

"Just pray for her to live a long and blessed life. I believe she has divine influence, and her prayers are being heard. Perhaps on her journey in life, God will use her as his instrument of love." The priest blessed us and asked Margaret to pray for him and pray for peace in the world.

I was puzzled by his remarks. What does God have in store for my little one?

Then I remembered one day I had sent Margaret over to an elderly sick lady to bring her some food. When Margaret came back home, she told me what the elderly woman had her do...

"Mama, she was sitting in a chair, and she said she couldn't move. She was all covered up, and said her legs pained her and she couldn't reach them. 'They're falling asleep' she said. 'Be a good child and rub them for me...please?' (Her legs were all wrinkled and they had sores on them.) I didn't want to touch them, but...I did, mama, I rubbed them and she gave out a shout, so I ran out of the house crying. I didn't meant to hurt her, honest, Mama, honest!"

I immediately went over to the elderly woman's house to see what had happened. On entering her home, I saw that the woman was standing, she looked perfectly fine. She smiled at me and told me of how Margaret had cured her. "Margaret is blessed. Your daughter has the touch of an angel...She touched my legs and she healed them."

When I left the woman, she was praising God, and thanking Him for her healing. (My Margaret did that?) I thought the woman must have been exaggerating, and I put it out of my mind.

Returning home exhausted from that experience, I was subject to another disclosure from my Aunt Irene. I received a letter from her, telling me of how bad Europe was getting. "Ellen and I are in the process of selling everything and starting a new life in Paris, France." She told me of how Ellen will set up her shop and when they were settled, "I will send you the rest of your estate money."

"Pray for us, Amelia, we need your prayers. Europe needs your prayers.

"I love you all, Jesus bless." Aunt Irene.

Again! I wrote back saying, "Please come here, you will be safe in America." But I'm afraid my plea fell on deaf ears.

Meanwhile, Stephen was turning 19 years old and graduating from high school. The wings of time quickly rushed by, for it was not too long ago Stephen was a boy. Now he is a man. There was an ache in my heart I cannot explain. Nevertheless, I wouldn't change anything for a moment. He was just like a son and I was proud of him. He worked at Colt's Manufacturing during the school years, and now he was a full-time employee with a good chance of advancement. Who wouldn't be proud of him.

J.J. was earning money so he could continue his violin lessons and buy a new violin. He said he wanted to be a musician with a band of his own.

My husband was being seen around town riding in an automobile. J.J. and Stephen said it was a Model K. Then Stephen, with his eyes widening, said, "It's a high cost car. It has a six cylinder – 7000 – cc with a large engine made in 1906."

I asked, "Stephen, how do you know so much about that car?"

"Papa told me, papa says she's got a Type 2 Surrey Rambler made in 1905, too."

"She, who's she?" They said they didn't know, only "she's an older woman with blonde hair."

"Oh," I said, "the car must belong to his boss." And dismissed any jealous feelings from creeping in.

The year was 1913, Thomas Woodrow Wilson was elected as the 28th President of the United States.

And that year I tried to get a job in an insurance company – I was told, "Immigrants need not apply, your English is good, but you have an accent. When you improve and lose it…come back."

Although that was not the first time I was discriminated against, I felt the sting much more since I had just graduated night college.

That's when I decided to take Mary Kelly up on her offer to cook and sew for some of her friends.

Alek was four and very hard to nail down. I had to keep him on a harness because he was always running away.

That year Amelia fell off a high fence and was in the hospital in traction for a week. Being six years of age in a body cast was a little difficult for both of us.

And...home for a few weeks, she almost drove me crazy.

But with the help of God and my good friends, we came through it all.

Where was Joseph, you ask? I had no idea. I hadn't heard or received any money from him in weeks. I inquired at his job and was told he had left.

Sometime later I received a letter from Joseph. The postmark read Arkansas. The letter started out, "Please forgive me, Amelia. Amelia, I had to get away, my life was getting too complicated. It was nothing you had done to me. It was what I was doing to you."

The letter continued, "I am now a ranchman again and breeding Blue Ribbon colts. I love it here, I wish I could send for you, but funds are low...I will send you some money as soon as I can. I put all my money into the ranch. Please don't hate me. I guess I never grew up. I will always love you forever; a kiss to all." Joseph.

My heart ached for him being so foolish. And his leaving hurt me, but leaving four minor children...grieved me more. The feeling of abandonment captured my soul. I felt a great loss as if he had died.

I prayed for consolation and found none. Even the voice of my papa saying, Amelia, everything will be all right, did not comfort me.

My children needed me now more than ever. My funds were low too. Stephen contributed most of his pay check. J.J. stopped taking violin lessons, but his teacher, Mr. Wilhelm Wileck, would not hear of it. "Joe (that's what he called him) has too much talent to stop." He told me, "Mrs. Tolda, I will tutor him for nothing." So he did!

I had to work in order for my family to survive. Yet I had to stay home with my younger children. So…what was I to do? Mary Kelly came to the rescue. She got me jobs with her friends, and their friends, and so on.

Therefore, I did all of my cooking at home and brought whole meals over to my new employers' houses.

But it was not all roses for me to be able to cook in the kitchen, I had to keep a harness on Alek. He sure was a handful. I used to tie him to the kitchen table, so I wouldn't step on him. Thank God, Margaret and Amelia helped me with Alek. They also helped me with the meals. Thank you, Jesus, for all your assistance, especially the love of my children.

I had a zest for life, and looked forward to the next day, with each one full of humor and spirit. Keeping busy was my refuge.

I started getting jobs from very wealthy people. I had so many offers, I had to turn some away. My prayers and tears were heard, my socks knew no bounds.

After a few months, sad news erupted from Europe. It was the 18th of June, 1914, the heir to Austria's throne was assassinated. Archduke Francis Fredinand and his wife, the Duchess of Hohenberg were killed by a terrorist organization. I read on…World War I begins when Austria declares war on Serbia.

1914 J.J. was 15 and had just paid
off his violin - all of $7.00 -
at 25¢ a week.
He taught Stephen to play - age 19.
And...every week-end they sounded
like a little bit of heaven.

My thoughts ran immediately to my Aunt Irene. I called Fiorello LaGuardia at his law office, hoping he could help get my aunt to America. Mr. LaGuardia informed me that, "Ellis Island was just about closed – just a trickle can come in. But I'll see what I can do."

On August 3rd, Germany declared war on France. I kept calling for help. I asked Captain Robert to speak to anyone he knew that had some influence.

He told me, "The United States strongly opposes participation in the conflict, even though US Maritime rights on the high seas were being violated. Authorities," he said, "would help if they could, but immigration has practically ceased."

August 30th – "First German air raid on Paris." I thought I would die when I read that headline. I immediately wired a counselor at the State Department in Paris. My worst fear came true.

I had learned that Auntie's building was destroyed in the bombing – and they were presumed dead. I fell on my knees and quivered with tears falling on the telegram I had just received.

My papa's voice called out to me again. "Amelia, everything will be all right, trust in Divine Providence. They are with our family – they're in heaven."

A great relief came over me, "Thank you, papa."

The next day a letter from my dear aunt came – three weeks before her death. She said they were on their way to Paris. Enclosed was a bank note. It was the rest of my estate. The bank note was for eight thousand dollars.

I was nervous handling that large sum and didn't know what to do with it.

Nervously I went to the bank and cashed the bank note. Ordinarily I would have deposited it. But my woman's intuition took over, and I went home and socked it away in my dresser drawer.

It was early in 1915 when I received a consolation card from Mr. LaGuardia for my aunt's untimely death. On an enclosed note, he wrote:

"My condolences, I know words cannot alleviate your pain. I had sad news also, my mother came to visit me from Budapest. She stayed with me for a few months then left for home. I was told she died a short time later, she was only 56. She had diabetes and was very sick. She knew she didn't have much time. I am grateful I had a chance to see her once again. God is good." LaGuardia.

I wrote back to him, saying, "Stay strong. That's how your mother would want it. Put everything in God's hands and trust in Him. I'm praying for you." Amelia.

It seemed everyone was in a sad state of mind.

It was May 23, 1915. Italy declared war on Austria-Hungary. The world is going crazy.

The following year, 1916, I received a short letter from the House of Representatives. It read:

"Thank you, Amelia, for all your prayers. You're right, my mother would be proud of me. Keep praying. It sure works. I was elected to Congress from the 14th District and I won by only 357 votes. Take care." LaGuardia.

That year I bought a two family brick house for $5,800 dollars on Wilson Street with my estate money. It had five rooms downstairs, five rooms on the second floor, and three rooms in the attic.

I had a sewing room, wonderful gardens, beautiful roses, and a cow named Youcee. And chickens that all had names.

But it was sad for us to eat them, so after awhile I stopped naming them. And you know what...they started to taste better after that.

I never brought a thing from the store except milk for Margaret. She would not drink Youcee's (the cow) milk.

This was a perfect house. I had a telephone installed, a six-foot American flag on a brass stand that I placed in the dining area. I crocheted a tablecloth with a pineapple design and soon I had a small business making them for my employers.

Then one day a knock came at the door. Standing there was my husband, Joseph. He was thin and poorly dressed. He didn't look like himself. I hardly recognized him. "Amelia, it's me," he said.

My heart went out to him. How could I turn him away? I still loved him.

He pleaded with me to stay and I allowed him in my home and into my heart...In a short time, I gave myself to him again.

And a new life came into our world. I was happy when Mary Barbara was born December 18, 1916. So was Joseph.

Joseph started working at Colt's Patent Firearms, at the Hartford Division. He was making very good money and things were going smooth.

Joseph was pleased with the Wilson house... and the new baby. He said he was sorry that I had to carry the load alone. "But Amelia, I'm here to stay. I love you and the children. I want another chance at happiness with my family."

Joseph seemed...sincere...

The first week in February, a note was pinned to my pillow. "I love you, Amelia, but family life is too much for me. I have gone to live with my sister. Sorry, please understand. Kiss the children for me." Joseph.

After that brief note, my life ended as a married woman. It was like falling into a deep pit and having to crawl out on my hands and knees. I cried a thousand tears and pledged to myself this will never happen to me again.

Out of the pit I came and brushed myself off and started all over again.

My son, J.J., informed me after his papa left, that he will be called Joe, never Joseph... "I'm Joe, remember, mama."

He was very hurt and couldn't understand why his papa left again. He was very distressed and at times thought it was his fault.

I tried to fill in the empty spaces where he had questions. But...I never knew if I did.

Then it happened! Big headlines. "April 6, 1917. US Declares War on Germany."

After the 16th of April, US troops landed in France.

Many died and among those brave men who died on foreign soil...was Captain Robert.

The letter from his wife was heartbreaking. Here was a man who loved his family and human kind with all his heart. And now he's gone.

"Oh, Captain Robert, you are now with your Heavenly Father."

Soon after, Mr. LaGuardia signed up for the Aviation section of the Signal Corp in April. He was commissioned 1st Lieutenant and then promoted to Captain. He was called the "First Flying Congressman." I was very proud of him.

My Joseph left us again, 2 months after
Mary Barbara was born in December, 1916
1917, Margaret age 14 holding Mary.

Wilson Street home - 1917.
Taken a few days after my 37th
birthday.
(left to right) Papa, J.J.
me, Margaret and Stephen.

Margaret age 15 - in native dress
won a dance contest at the
Hungarian Club in Hartford, Ct..
She danced the Csardas - (1918).

On November 7th, Joe turned 18, and after December 7, 1917, the US declared war on Austria.

"Mama," Joe said, "Mr. LaGuardia joined the service, and so am I. I want to fight for this country because I love America. I must go...Stephen said he's going too."

Christmas came! New Years went. Another year of emotional prayers were sent up to heaven.

It seemed everyone was praying for peace. Churches were packed. Mothers were in tears. Flags in the windows with stars showed who were killed. Son... husband... brother.

My heart ached for all of them. "Oh God, am I to lose my sons to this horrible war too?"

Joe knew my anguish and promised me he would wait till he was 19. Stephen, knowing how I felt, encouraged Joe to keep his promise.

The Nation's prayers were answered.

November 11, 1918...Armistice Day.

Peace at last!

Chapter 15

All My Children

We all came down with a bout of influenza the end of 1918, except for Margaret, she remained free of the disease. Thank God for that because she was able to take care of us.

So at the start of the New Year we awaited a promising 1919, even though it took awhile for me to bounce back from our illness. The influenza left me weak at times and I tired easily.

As fate would have it…my good friend Anna pitched in to help me get back on my feet so I wouldn't lose my cooking jobs. When she helped around the kitchen, she would tell me so many interesting stories about her life in Russia.

She remembers when Lenin arrived in Moscow from Switzerland in April, 1917. "Everyone" she said, "was so frightened of him, they said he was a devil. The Bolsheviks took away our land and seized power. They began a reign of terror against us.

"People were starving, and I remember the night the Red Army came to take my father to fight for them. We hid him in the barn under a stack of hay. Afterwards we literally abandoned everything and left with just the clothes on our backs.

"We made our way to Minsk, White Russia. Then to the border of Poland, where my mother's cousins lived. They were to help us get to the Baltic Sea. There we were to board a steamship to Sweden."

Anna started to cry. "My family didn't make it. The night we were to sail, they were all killed by spies belonging to the Red Army. Just my sister and I escaped and made our way to Britain.

"The Civil War between the Bolsheviks (the Red Army) and anti-Bolsheviks (the White Army) was still going strong when we emigrated to America.

"I thank God for America every day," she said.

I hugged Anna and said, "Forget the past miseries, only remember your good times with your loved ones. Keep only important memories that make you happy. God wants your happiness, so don't disappoint Him."

August was here so soon, and my Margaret was turning sixteen. I arranged to have a birthday party and invite all her friends. I had a whole watermelon for her, just like I promised (Margaret was crazy about watermelon), but alas, Margaret was locked in her bedroom all that night nursing a whopper of a toothache. So...her friends ate her watermelon.

When Amelia turned thirteen in April, 1920, she had discovered boys. She would always be fixing her hair and sneaking lip rouge. And she would always be singing (she had a beautiful voice). Mary, who would be four in December, had to clap when Amelia finished her act, or else. Amelia proclaimed she was going to be a movie star and practiced how to smile in the mirror every day. I told her, "Amelia, at least you look happy, keep smiling." Mary started to mimic her. Now I had two stars to contend with, so far no cracked mirrors, just dirty fingerprints.

Alek was an ordinary boy of eleven, very mischievous, full of life and always laughing. His prankish ways gave me some concern at times. But his kindness and thoughtfulness made me forgive his shortcomings.

Joe had been praised by the newspapers as a young newcomer bandleader. He played at The Bond Hotel in Hartford and was a "smash" whatever that means.

Stephen bought an automobile that following year. I believe it was a 1925 Ford Model T (nicknamed the "Tin Lizzie"). Stephen said the top speed was 40 mph, so I better get something to tie my hair down or else it might blow away. Anyway I didn't believe him...We made plans to take a long overdue vacation and "test the speed." I needed this trip very badly and jumped at the chance in spite of the fact I may lose my hair.

Our first trip was to Ridgefield, Connecticut.

Stephen knew I loved American History, so we started out in Ridgefield, a town that revered history.

We saw historic buildings from the Revolutionary War. Where Benedict Arnold was made a Major General by an Act of Congress for gallantry.

I asked, "Wasn't he the American General who became a traitor and fled to the British side?"

I heard a thunderous, "Yes."

Then I read an inscription as follows:

In Defense of American Independence at the Battle of Ridgefield, April 17, 1777 -- Died -- Eight Patriots Who were laid in these grounds – companioned by Sixteen British soldiers.

167

-- Living their Enemies –
-- Dying their Guests –
In honor of Service and Sacrifice.

How sad that was to read…Yet the pain I felt in my heart was not only for them, but for myself also.

I felt like my husband was another…Benedict Arnold, betraying me to the world. Plus the humiliation I had felt and the dishonor he brought to the family and the pain he caused his children.

Then I read on:

"This memorial is placed for the Strengthening of Hearts."

The words "Strengthening of Hearts" tugged at my spirit. My pain will always be a part of me, the pain of loss! Like these brave young men on both sides, I too will be brave.

Riding home I was so inspired that I made an oath to do something for this country's wonderful people.

Days later I got in touch with the local Catholic charities. "What can I do for the community?" I asked. In a blink of an eye I had a job…I had agreed to take in wayward girls and house them until their delivery time.

One day Margaret, on seeing the full-bellied girls, asked, "Mama, how come they're all so fat?"

So as not to embarrass the all ready self-conscious girls, I took Margaret aside and answered, "These girls are hungry and I'm feeding them."

"They don't look hungry to me, mama," she said.

That's when I had a heart to heart talk to Margaret about the "Birds and Bees."

That night her enlightenment came and Margaret was changed from adolescence to grown-up.

After school Margaret got a job in a department store in the tube room department as a cashier. She was a wizard at mathematics.

With her first paycheck she bought a pale green hat with a matching scarf. When she brought it home, she said, "Try it on, mama, see if you like it."

I said out loud, "Oh, it looks so pretty on me." Then I blushed for shame, how conceited.

"It's yours, mama, I bought it for you."

"For me?" I said, and kissed her lovely face. It was times like this my struggles all seemed worth it.

I felt appreciated and much loved. I wore the pale green hat and the matching scarf everywhere...even to work (after all I made my own clothes, and this was a treat for me).

Mary, almost five, wanted to wear the pale green hat and the matching scarf. She thought it was a badge of honor. I finally had to put it away.

Mary hung on me like a clinging vine. Her papa had not seen her since she was two, but she kept asking for him.

How sad, there my husband had a child he didn't want to see...and Fiorello LaGuardia would have done anything to have his daughter with him. He lost his beloved child, Fioretta, not even one year old to tuberculosis meningitis on May 8, 1921.

On hearing this news of his infant's premature death, I sent him a letter:

"Dear Fiorello, 'Just have faith,' I told him of my little Leslie and said, "Life would be different for you. It will change for the better if...only you could come to accept your grief. These are not just words, Fiorello, it's a fact. I speak from experience. My life changed. My love for my baby will never die. My heart, that once had an empty spot, is now filled with love, love for others. My baby lives in them."

I told him, "I am content right now, knowing that my Joe is a prominent violinist. So, on his 22nd birthday, I bought him a Stradivarious violin for $500 from a gypsy that lived in Buffalo, New York, who came from Rumania. No kidding, it's true.

"He was a friend of a friend. Whom by the way I hardly knew, but I believe in fate and Joe was meant to have this wonderful violin. It was a beauty and Joe worshipped it.

"Joe played for the first time on that sweet sounding instrument for his family. Margaret played the piano, Stephen the viola, and Alek the drums. Amelia, Mary and I sang. We had our own home concert. You must come next time.

"I'll close with prayers for you." Your friend, Amelia.

That year went by fast, but it was a good year for Joe. He played with such orchestras' as Bill Tasillo's Cinderella Ballroom Orchestra, and Emil Heimberger's Hotel Bond Orchestra.

The peak of his musical experience was attained when he was signed by Jean Goldkette. People still speak fondly about the greatest, All-Star combination in the history of swing. It included:

Bix Beiderbecke, Hoagy Carmichael of "Star Dust" fame; Tommy and Jimmy Dorsey; Saxophonist Frankie Trumbauer; fiddler Joe Venuti; drummer Gene Krupa; trombonist Bill Rank; and clarinetist, Pee Wee Russell.

Joe stayed with the band for a year and then decided that he needed to earn more money. So he attended the University with the help of the sock money I had stashed in

J.J. taken in 1921 on his 22nd birthday.
With his new love - a Stradivarious violin.
That week he played with the Hotel Bond
Orchestra.

the dresser drawer. Over the years I kept adding to it, always promising to put it in the bank and receive some interest. Oh well, one of these days I'll do it.

Joe got a job with the Travelers Insurance Company at the home office on the group staff, after classes.

He still played at the Travelers dances and was a hit with the gals.

Everything was going fine for us, but not at Fiorello's home, for Death struck again. His beloved wife, Thea, died on November 29th. She was only twenty-six.

I sent a Mass card of condolence and kept him in my prayers. Fiorello took her death hard, but I knew he'd pull through with God's help.

Then January, 1922, I received a card introducing a new law firm – LaGuardia, Sapinsky & Amster.

And a note: Thank you for your support and prayers. It worked again. God bless and keep praying. By the way, Amelia, I'm taking your advice. I'm filling that empty spot in my heart with lots of love. I want to make a difference in this sad world. Thanks again. LaGuardia.

His note of confidence inspired me to help the heavyhearted. I set up a soup kitchen and also went to work on making clothes for the less fortunate that come to my door for help.

Thoughts of Sister Mary came to my mind. I could just see her smiling at me and saying again, "Everyone has a task to do. You are a light in the world, let it shine so other's will give glory to the Father because of you...and your love."

Then in my mind she reminded me of Samuel in the Bible. "Here I am, Lord, I come to do Your Will."

Also my old saying still applies. "He that gives, gets." And...I was being blessed, for my baking jobs paid well. My dresser drawer now had lots of fat socks.

Margaret was saving up also, she wanted to buy me a fur coat and surprise me for my birthday next February (but her little sister, Mary, couldn't keep this secret).

Nineteen twenty-three was upon us. I received my fur coat and...I was so...surprised!

My little Mary was to make her First Holy Communion. It was time to dig into the trunk in the attic and retrieve the dress that Margaret wore for her encounter with the Lord.

I bought Mary a gold cross necklace and I sewed live flowers on the top of her veil. She had white shined shoes with two straps across the arch and white nylon stockings.

I sent an invitation to her papa and had the camera man all set to take a family portrait. Papa didn't show up for Mary's great occasion. Neither did any of his side of the family.

Five years and she had not laid eyes on her papa. How tragic...for both of them.

Instead of a family portrait, I settled for snapshots.

That summer, Hartford was sweltering in the heat, the children clambered to go to New London Beach, so after a slight uproar and wearing me down, we were on our way.

I had brought a new swim suit with a bright skirt and a bright matching bathing hat – and black stocking to the calf. (In hopes it would hide my varicose veins). And I thought I was the cat's meow. That was until I saw the pictures I had taken at the beach. I laughed so hard at the funny looking me.

My life was happy, yet lonely. Thank you, Jesus, for my good children. I miss Joseph. Am I foolish? Maybe lonely?

It was October of 1925, around 6:00 a.m. when a vigorous knocking at the door woke me up. To my surprise, it was Julia. Had something happened to Joseph? My heart came up to my throat and throbbed rapidly.

She greeted me with a warm smile. "Did I wake you?" she said with a wide Cheshire grin. Then like a streak of lightning, her face changed. "I need your help, Amelia."

Before I could ask what's wrong, she began to cry, saying that her husband had lost his job and they were up to their neck in debt. She said she came to borrow $1,500. I didn't say a word, I just raised my eyebrow.

"You can't turn me down," she said. "I know you have it. Alek told his papa that you have a drawer full of money."

"Julia," I said, "when did Alek see his papa?"

"He saw him every weekend for the last three months," she answered.

I asked, "Why was this kept a secret? I should have been told that he was seeing his papa. What questions did you ask my son? Why did he tell you I had money in the drawer? How did that come about?"

Julia's evasion of my questions were apparent. She unmasked herself only slightly. "Joseph just questioned him about you, and what you were doing. It's all innocent. Won't you please help me? I'll pay you back with interest, please."

I examined her face, her wrinkled brow, and the sad exasperated look in her eyes. My pity for her prompted me to give in. "Wait here," I said, and foolishly came back with the money.

When Alek awoke, I too questioned him. "Alek, why didn't you tell me you were seeing your papa?"

Alek rubbed his tired eyes and said, "Aunt Julia and papa told me not to tell you. If I did, you would never speak to me again. So I was afraid to tell you."

"Alek, what kind of questions did they ask you?"
Slipping into his shoes, he said, "They asked me if you had a man sleeping in the attic, and if I ever saw you kiss that man."

"What did you tell them, Alek?"

"I said, no. You only kiss us children. Mama, can I have breakfast now? I'm hungry."

I continued to ask Alek more questions at the breakfast table. I learned that Julia asked most of the questions.

Alek said that most of the questions had to do with the men that were seen coming and going from the house.

"Alek? Alek? Didn't you tell her they were hungry, and I fed them on the porch and sent them on their way, and that no one came in the house?"

"No, mama! She didn't give me a chance to speak."

"Alek? Did you tell them I work for the charities, and they send people over to me to feed? Did you tell them that?"

"Yes, mama, I did. Aunt Julia said I was becoming a mama's boy. That I should grow up. And papa said he wants me to live with him so he can make a man out of me."

Alek started to cry. "I said yes when papa asked me to live with him."

"You want to leave home? You're only sixteen, Alek, you're still in school. Why? Why?" I asked. "Are you not treated good here? What did papa offer you? Wait! Don't tell me. If you want to go, then go! When you're ready to come home, come."

I kissed him and turned away swiftly so he could not see my tears.

In less than two weeks, Alek came back home, promising never to leave me again. This time I asked no questions, I just hugged him tenderly, saying, "Welcome home, son."

Everything slid back to normal, and we went on from there. No looking back...eyes to the future.

Margaret had vacation time coming up, and Mary Banks (her best friend) talked Margaret into visiting her cousin in New York City.

After Margaret's vacation time ended, she still kept going to New York City. I found out from her that she had met a young man and was quite taken with him.

The young man came to Connecticut at a special invitation of mine. He was a tall, blonde, slender-built man with a smile that would never quit. He displayed a great sense of humor. He laughed at all my jokes (that was a plus). I could see he made my Margaret happy. That's all I ever wanted for her.

I noticed Stephen was very jealous and a bit angry when he was introduced to James, Margaret's new beau.

I found out later that he too had fallen in love with Margaret. But, of course, Margaret always thought of him as a big brother.

Margaret, now 22, informed me that she had accepted a great job in New York and would stay with Mary

Margaret, love struck at the tender
age of 22.

My precious Grandson Jimmy,
18½ months old (1929).
Who kept me on my toes every
summer.
"Gam-mama please bake a cake
for me." He would say in that
cute New York accent...
Who could resist him...?

Bank's cousin. She said she wanted to be near her young man and thought this was the real thing. Love...

I gave her my blessings and sent a message with my love to James, saying, "Remember, James, God is watching you and so am I..."

After a year courtship, Margaret and James married. It was a small but wonderful wedding, family and friends and lots of love. I was happy at her choice.

Amelia was the next to marry. Now I had two wonderful sons-in-law.

I remember one weekend Margaret and her new husband drove up from New York in their convertible (with the top down) with a gift for me.

It was a yellow canary bird in a gold cage. They put it in the back seat of the car. By the time they got to my home, the poor bird had lost all of its feathers on its head. He was still adorable, and oh, could he sing. Even my cats loved him.

Then the unthinkable happened right after Margaret went back to New York. I was summoned to court. Julia brought a civil action against me for harassment.

She claimed I had pursued her relentlessly for the money she had borrowed from me and declared that she had paid me every last dime...ages ago.

The truth was she never did pay me a cent and I had never asked her for it...Why was she doing this?

On the stand she said terrible things about me and my character. And made a statement that Joe and Margaret were not her brother's children.

The lawsuit made a claim for my home, saying that her brother Joseph paid for the home, and she helped him. Joseph sat there not saying a word.

Margaret stood up and said, "Your Honor, look at my father, and now look at me. I have his blue eyes, and I do look like him. How can he deny that I'm not his?"

The Judge looked at them both and nodded his head in the affirmative.

"Margaret, please sit down," I said. I then asked the Judge if I may speak. Again he nodded yes.

I stood up and said, "Your Honor, I am being demoralized. I would like the chance to respond by having my lawyer get in touch with Mr. LaGuardia in New York City. He will be able to get a hold of the manifestos taken at Ellis Island. In that document it will state that my husband, Joseph, swore the children brought to America were his children."

The Judge recessed until the papers could be obtained.

When the court resumed, I was exonerated on both... accusations. Julia wound up paying for legal and court fees. And...was told to reimburse me for the loan.

I walked past Joseph, his head bent low. I leaned over and whispered in his ear, "Joseph, I forgive you."

I put all that unpleasantness behind me and went on with my life.

My first grandchild was born to Margaret on October 17, 1927. I was delirious with joy. And my Margaret looked radiant as she held her little boy and pressed a kiss on his cheek.

I wrote to Joseph and told him that he was now a grandfather, that Margaret had a beautiful blond-haired baby with big blue eyes. "Just like yours, Joseph! Strange how truth always pokes its head up, doesn't it, Joseph?"

My charities were having a meeting in Washington, D.C., in the autumn of 1928, and I was chosen to be the spokesman for a group of Connecticut ladies on "The Dignity of Life in America."

What an honor...I felt so humble.

At the podium a lump gathered in my throat. I spoke about being an immigrant, and how hard it was for some to accept me. I said, "I met discrimination head on. I was a foreigner with a funny accent. Someone to laugh at. And, to some I was an intruder. But with the majority of people I met, I found there was less bigotry and more love. And it was because of them I became strong. I tried to do my best to be a role model to my children and grandchildren, and to all immigrants.

"Opportunities were given to me to better myself. I was able to go to night school, and it was difficult. I received a degree in English and Social Science. I took advantage of all the possibilities that America provided to all of her people.

"The Lady in the Harbor had her arm outstretched to light the way for me. I could not let her down. She told me I could be anyone I wished to be.

"Being a woman, a mother and a Catholic in this day and age takes commitment, fortitude, strength of character and courage.

"My papa, God rest his soul, always said to me, 'Be of good heart, then Amelia, everything will be all right.'"

Chapter 16

My Reward

December 1928, a rather cold wind and snow blew in just before Christmas, but it felt very festive. Our tree was decorated with flashing lights and the tinsel glittered like diamonds on a...very tall tree.

Alek was seeing a lovely girl who to my surprise was only sixteen. Alek was nineteen and acted like thirty.

He told me he was very much in love and wanted to get married. "You're much too young for marriage, and so is she," I said. "When you're older, I'll make sure you have a grand wedding. Just give yourself time to be friends first."

A week later Alek said they had to get married because she was in the family way. They ran off without my blessings. I was hurt that he didn't trust his heart with me anymore.

After the elopement, Alek came to me almost crying. "I cannot lie to you anymore, mama. Lou is not going to have a baby. She is a good girl and I loved her so much. I thought that this was the only way you would approve."

"Tush, tush, that's how much you know, my son. I told you, Alek, that you would have a grand wedding. So let's do this right, son." And a grand wedding we had! I baked a wedding cake with five tiers. And the bride and groom were made out of candy that I molded and painted with food color. The flowers were made out of pastry and confectioners' sugar. This was the best tasting cake I ever made. Oh, I forgot, I also put a lot of love in it.

I told my little boy while dancing with him, "Alek, trust in those who love you, confide in them, and you'll be real surprised. I too loved at a young age but I did not let time do its job. Remember, time can be a friend if you let it. Don't always be in a hurry."

That Christmas, my home was packed with all my loved ones. What better present could I receive...love was here.

Then came a year I will never forget, 1929.

Herbert Hoover was elected the 31st President of the United States. Most people felt he was right for this high office, since he headed the Food Administration and War Relief Bureaus during and after World War I. He helped destitute farmers and recommended extensive public works. But, nothing seemed to help. It was the beginning of hard times for most Americans.

The "Market Crash" of October 1929 started the "Great Depression" in the United States. It was awful. People were committing suicide by jumping off bridges and out of windows. Factories were shut down. So many people lost their jobs and their homes. The bank officials had a hard time trying to control riots of people wanting their money back.

Insanity took over. It was like Satan had gotten loose roaming the world and seeking to devour anyone in His path.

But America was not alone in this "Great Depression." It was a global catastrophe.

The sock money I had stashed away in the dresser drawer was a God-send. I did...believe in banks, but I was glad I didn't trust them this time.

Joe and Stephen kept their jobs, but they cut back on their hours. They barely made a decent pay check.

Amelia and her husband Ray, and Alek and his wife Lou, came to stay with us. Rents were high and food was scarce.

Growing our own food, and having a new brown cow and lots of chickens made life bearable. Thank you, Jesus.

I was able to feed anyone who came to my door. No one was turned away.

Joseph, my husband, lost his job and all the money he had in the bank. His sister, Julia, asked him to leave, suggesting he return home. With no where to go, he came to me.

I gave him a room in the attic. He had his own bathroom and hot meals were served to him every day.

Our son Joe was angry with me for taking him in. He threatened to leave home if he stayed. "He's taking advantage of you, mama. Can't you see he doesn't love us, he never did? He's a user. He'll throw us away when he doesn't need us anymore."

"Joe, come here, sit by me," I said. "And think of what I'm saying to you..."

Joe came over and sat by me, putting his arms around me. "What is it, mama?"

"Son, I remember a verse in the Bible, it goes like this:

"Kindness to a father can wipe away a multitude of sins."

"Joe..." I squeezed him tightly, "forgive him, and you'll be forgiven. Find it in your heart, he's weak, Joe, and easily led. He does love you and he loves us. In his own way, he does."

Joe looked at me square in the eye, and said, "He denied he was my father and Margaret, also. So how can you ask me to do this?" He sobbed, walking away, saying, "But for you, mama, I will forgive him, and I'll try to love him once more. Just for you, mama."

I pray you will, my son, were my very thoughts.

I stayed cheerful by keeping busy and trying to make life easier. I always tried to laugh and light a candle, remembering, "This too shall pass."

Our charities were all overloaded and it seemed my share of hungry families increased every week.

I still had my job with the wealthy people in society. Baking cakes was my specialty, especially cheese cakes for the Governor. I cooked as if there were no depression.

Many times I was allowed to bring the left-overs home for my families, and I did…it was needed and much appreciated.

Hard times fell on Margaret and James. They just had a new baby, November 18, 1929. My new grand-daughter Barbara. She was beautiful with long black hair. I never saw so much hair on a newborn. She had violet eyes and creamy skin.

James worked as a rigger on buildings. He didn't want to leave New York and come to Connecticut for fear of not finding a job here. I told Margaret that they could live here rent free. But James refused the offer.

"You're too proud, James," I said. "Charity means love, and there's nothing wrong with helping someone you care about."

James thanked me and said, "It's evident how much you care for us, let me think about it, ma, all right?"

James was a very proud man and felt he had to do it on his own, so I left it at that.

It was wonderful with my Joseph home with us once again. I used to fantasize that he was my Rudolph Valentino (my favorite movie star) and I was his leading lady in the movie "The Sheik."

But as time went on, I realized my life with Joseph was just a fantasy. It was obvious Joseph was only interested in his own gratification. He did not promise me anything, nor try to assure me he would not leave again. And when his advances towards me failed, my husband moved back with his sister Julia...again.

But before he left, I tried to get him to tell me why he acted like a stranger towards his children. He shrugged his shoulders and said he didn't know.

I took his hand in mine and said, "Come back when you do know, Joseph. We'll be here." And I slowly shut the door behind him.

In my mind I realized that this separation would be our last farewell. "God be with you, Joseph."

My life was taken up with my grandson, Jimmy. He brightened my day and made each waking hour easier. He was my pride and joy.

When we visited Margaret in New York City, she let Jimmy come back with us for the summer, then every summer after that.

Amelia use to pretend Jimmy was hers. She treated him like he was one of her play dolls. She used to say to him, "What does the dolly do?" Then he would blink his eyes in rapid successive movements. Then Amelia would reward him with a cookie.

Amelia and Mary fought over who would feed him and carry him. But when it came time to change his diapers, well then...he was mine.

When I baked a cake for my employers, I would have to bake a small coconut cake, just for Jimmy.

He had a cute New York accent that beat my Hungarian one. I laughed all the time with him. I love him so.

Margaret had another child in April of 1931 and I asked her to name her Margaret...for me.

She almost lost this little one. Thank God she didn't. She was a premature baby, weighing only four pounds. She had to be fed with an eye dropper because her mouth was so tiny. She was born with a veil over her face, and when it was removed, she had peaches and cream skin. She was a beauty.

Margaret had another baby girl the following year. That meant four little mouths to feed. So I went into my miracle sock drawer and sent them some money.

In 1933 Amelia had a little boy, my second grandson, Billy. If I thought Amelia was possessive of her nephew Jimmy... She was worse with Billy. I hardly got a chance to hold him. Couldn't blame her though, he was handsome.

I loved them all. There's something about grandchildren you have to experience to know. It's a love, surpassing love.

That moment in time was not all joy. For it was estimated that twelve million men and women were out of work. Personal savings were wiped out for most poor souls.

Corporate bankruptcies and bank failures were common. Relief for the unemployed came from our charities and local governments.

I voted this time for Franklin D. Roosevelt. And it was like a breath of fresh air. He made work projects called the "New Deal." We held our breaths.

James got a job with the "Public Works Programs." That enabled Margaret and her family to get off of city relief...James had his dignity restored.

Joe was a full-time law student with three more years to go. I was very proud of him. He hadn't married yet, but had a car-full of gals after him

"When I become a lawyer," he said, "Mama, you won't have all these jobs. I'll have people waiting on you for a change." He constantly wanted me to quit my baking job. He said, "Your charity work is enough to do."

To me it was not work, it was a pleasure to see those happy faces, especially when they bit into one of my cakes.

On a cold winter November day, I was getting ready to deliver my bakery goodies to the mayor's house. Stephen and his wife Sara were waiting to drive me there, and...I was in a hurry. Tonight I was to help with their Thanksgiving preparations. It was to be a big gala occasion. Everybody that was anybody would be there. I guess politics had a hand in it. (Elections were coming up soon.)

The snow covered the icy walkway, and...rushing to the car, my footing caught a patch of the ice and down I went. I hit the back of my head so hard that it rendered me unconscious. I was carried back into the house and placed in my bed. I regained consciousness and insisted I wasn't hurt, but still a doctor was summoned and gave me a clean bill of health. So realizing the time and all those people that were waiting for me, I jumped up from the bed and rushed to have Stephen take me to the mayor's house.

I had terrible headaches since my fall on the ice. It got so bad that I would black out, and sometimes I would see double. This condition lasted until the following year. I recognized the signs and knew it was serious.

It was early in December when the doctors decided to hospitalize me. I fell into a coma and stayed that way for days on end.

Funny though, in spite of being in a coma, I heard everything that went on.

I had many visitors, but this one particular day I had a special visitor.

It was Julia.

No one was in the room but her and I. She came over and touched my hand. "Amelia, can you hear me? It's Julia."

She waited awhile...I could see her searching my face for a reaction from me. Then she burst into tears. "Please forgive me, I hurt you so much through the years. I poisoned Joseph's mind about you, and he believed me.

"I lied to my husband and children about you. I made the children stay away from you, even though I knew you loved them." She stopped talking...dead silence could be felt. She searched my face...

Then she started again, her eyes fixed on me. "Amelia, I made you out to be a nasty person, when, in fact, I'm the nasty one." She kissed me, her hot tears spilled over on me.

"Please don't' die. I betrayed you many times. I want to make it all up to you. Please get well...please?"

She lifted her eyes to heaven, "Oh God, tell me it's not too late." She shook my hand rapidly. "Do you hear me...Amelia?"

She leaned down to my ear and whispered. "Amelia. I was always jealous of you and your goodness. Promise me, Amelia, when you get to heaven, you'll pray for me, and you'll forgive me. Do this so I won't be damned in the everlasting infernal."

She left the room so distraught my heart went out to her. But...I could not speak, my eyes were closed...., yet I could see her. "I forgive you, Julia, go in peace," were my thoughts.

Then Joseph came in. He bent down and kissed my cold lips, saying, "I love you, I always have, forgive me. Why did I treat you so badly? You were always so kind to me. Kind to everyone. I should be here, not you..." he left the room a broken man.

"Joseph, I wish you could hear me. I forgive you, and I'll always love you."

My family came and gathered all around me, the good sisters from the charities were there saying the rosary. Everyone was there, except my Margaret.

"Look!" someone said, "Amelia smiled."

I did smile...I was happy she was not here. I wanted to spare my Margaret from seeing me like this. Memories of my Margaret penetrated my thoughts. So many things happened to her. When she was seven she was running to see her new baby brother Alek and tripped and split her head open in two places. The doctor sewed her up in the house without any anesthetic.

She told me later that her guardian angel was holding her hand, that's why she didn't cry...And when she was thirteen, she was playing in the fields and while climbing over a fence, she became frightened by a garden snake and fell off and fractured her arm, it separated in two places, and was just hanging there. A stranger passing by helped her.

This stranger was a black man that showed up out of nowhere (his face was very bright and he smiled all the time). He broke a branch off a tree and placed it on her severed arm, then tied it up with his shirt that he had torn off his back, and said, "Go straight home, Margaret!" The doctor said if that stranger didn't come by, she would have lost her arm. Margaret always said, "The stranger was an angel, because when he stood next to me, I felt peaceful, and electricity radiated from him...and he knew my name."

Plus the ordeal we both had to go through when she fractured her neck.

Oh how I love her...I was blessed.

I loved all my children, but I must confess I had a sneaky feeling for my Margaret.

Then I started to feel strange, the coldness was leaving me. My eyes were clouded, and the voices were muffled, everything seemed in a distance.

The room was growing darker and darker.

But...I felt warm...? I felt wonderful...

That day December 19, 1935...I died.

An angel came to me. He stretched out his hand, "Take hold," he said.

I pleaded with the angel, "Oh, please not yet, I can't go yet. I must do something first, please wait. It's my Margaret, I must comfort her.

The angel understood and nodded yes. "Do what you must do," he said, "but hurry. The Light is waiting for us, we cannot be too long. We must go to The Light, hurry."

I was waked in my home. I watched them file by me, crying and touching my hand.

The doorbell rang and Alek said, "That must be Margaret, someone stand behind her when she faints."

I immediately went through...the closed door and whispered to my Margaret, "Don't cry, my little one.

"My joy will last forever."

I knew she heard me, because I touched her soul and she was calm.

Now my task was finished.... I was ready for The Light, but it did not come...I was allowed to stay a little longer.

Margaret came over to my casket, a hush came over the room. She kissed my hand and said, "Mama, my baby was critically ill. I couldn't come any sooner."

I could see her big tears dropping. She whispered to me, "I asked a priest to tell me what I should do. He said 'Stay with your sick child, that's what your mama would have done.'

"Was he right, Mama?"

I whispered softly, "Yes..."

Margaret held my hand, "Mama, I love you so much, forgive me for the times I hurt you. I'll miss you..."

I saw the pain in her face. I caressed her again, "Everything will be all right, my sweet Margaret...go in peace. I love you too."

Margaret stood up and blessed herself, then sat with her siblings.

I couldn't believe all the flowers and people that came. Even the All-Star Jazz Band was there playing my favorite songs.

Someone said, "Amelia was a true American." Then someone...took the American flag that was standing in the corner of my dining room and draped my coffin with it.

Oh, I felt wonderful...

A letter was read, "Keep praying for me when you're in heaven, Amelia. I need your prayers.

"Your devoted friend, Fiorello."

My thoughts were... I will pray for you all. Oh, how I will miss you all. But don't be sad for I am truly happy.

...A joy that will last forever.

There was a long motorcade to my interment. The flag...was still draped on my coffin.

The Honor Guard from the capitol saluted me when I passed by.

Me...? Just an immigrant.

I stayed with Margaret, Amelia and Mary right by their side. They even said they felt my presence.

Joe, Stephen and Alek looked so brave, and very sad. My little men...I'm proud of you all...stay strong.

Joseph was there and placed a rose on my coffin. I kissed his cheek and murmured, "I love you, Joseph."

And Julia, she was there, her head bent low, and crying.

Margaret put her arms around papa and said, "Mama would want me to love you...for her. I forgive you, papa,"

Joe came over to papa and kissed him. "Mama said I should love you again, I'll try, papa, I'll try." They both walked off with their arms around papa. I smiled.
After the priest blessed me, they lowered me into the ground.

I was laid to rest two days before Christmas.

Now...! I will see my Savior.

My angel said, "It's time, Amelia, they're all waiting for you."

I walked towards the warm Light and was greeted by my mama and papa, and all my siblings, my two little baby angels (My first child and Leslie)

And... Auntie and Uncle Albert and Ellen and of course, my friends Elizabeth and Captain Robert.

And dear sweet Sister Mary, she said, "Well done, my child, you listened well..."

There were angels singing:

This is not your ending, but...just your beginning

They were chanting and cymbals were clashing...beating...a musical...ringing sound.

It rang out: Amelia...Enter...

...You were...A light in the world...

...You let a light shine before men...

...Seeing your good works, they gave Glory to God...

...And...you gave to him that asked of thee...

...And...from him that would borrow from thee

...You turned not away...

...Yours is the Kingdom of Heaven.

Enter... Amelia...